It might almost be said that the most enchanting part of baseball lies not in watching it, but in remembering it. No sport lends itself so effortlessly to memory, to conversation; no sport has so graphic an afterlife in its statistics; nor has any been photographed so thoroughly and excitingly.

Beginning with 1901, the year most historians identify as the dawn of baseball's "modern era," there have been nearly 90 seasons, with no two even remotely alike. The mention of a certain year can evoke the memory of a team, the image of a man, or the drama of a moment. For many fans, it is all so vivid that baseball has become for them a long calendar of historical events.

Every season begins the same, with everyone equal on Opening Day, stirring with optimism and anticipation. And every season ends the same way, with surprises and disappointments, among teams and individuals both. No baseball summer has even been, or can be, dull. No baseball summer has ever been forgotten, for every one has been a source of stories and numbers, many of which have become part of our national folklore.

It is the purpose of this series of books to make it all happen one more time.

The Bantam
Baseball Collection
#6

Great
All-Star
Games

Written by
Bill Gutman

Packaged by Angel Entertainment, Inc.
and M.I.B. Baseball Enterprises, Inc.

BANTAM BOOKS
NEW YORK · TORONTO · LONDON · SYDNEY · AUCKLAND

Great All-Star Games

A Bantam Book/July 1989

All rights reserved
Copyright © 1989 by Angel Entertainment, Inc.
and M.I.B. Baseball Enterprises, Inc.
Cover photographs and interior photographs
copyright © 1989 The Card Memorabilia Associates, Ltd.

Book design/production by Karen J. Stelzl

No part of this book may be reproduced or transmitted
in any form or by any means, electronic or mechanical,
including photocopying, recording, or by any information
storage and retrieval system, without permission in
writing from the publisher.
For information address: Bantam Books.

ISBN 0-553-28024-4

Bantam Books are published by Bantam Books, a division of Bantam Doubleday Dell Publishing Group, Inc. Its trademark, consisting of the words "Bantam Books" and the portrayal of a rooster, is Registered in U.S. Patent and Trademark Office and in other countries. Marca Registrada, Bantam Books, 666 Fifth Avenue, New York, New York, 10103.

PRINTED IN THE UNITED STATES OF AMERICA

O   0 9 8 7 6 5 4 3 2 1

Contents

Introduction	1
The 1950 Game	5
The 1952 Game	17
The 1955 Game	25
The 1959 and 1960 Games	35
The 1961 Game	44
The 1964 Game	55
The 1967 Game	63
The 1968 Game	71
The 1970 Game	78
The 1971 Game	86
The 1972 Game	95
The 1979 Game	104
The 1983 Game	112
The 1984 and 1986 Games	120
The 1987 Games	130
Conclusion	138

Introduction

It's surprising that no one thought up the All-Star Game sooner. Since the American League was created to join the National League in 1903, the two leagues competed only in the pre-season and World Series. Yet with all the great stars of those early years, an All-Star Game would have been natural. How could baseball fans have resisted a game that would have matched Cobb against Wagner, Johnson against Mathewson, Sisler against Terry, or Babe Ruth against the entire National League?

But it wasn't until 1933 that Arch Ward, then the sports editor of the *Chicago Tribune*, proposed a contest between the National and American Leagues. The game was to be a fans' game—the teams would be chosen by them. Originally, it would be a single game—a dream game—played at the Chicago's Century of Progress Exposition scheduled to take place in the Windy City that summer. But, it didn't take long for the lords of baseball to jump on the All-Star bandwagon. Ward took the idea of a dream game to Baseball Commissioner Kenesaw Mountain Landis for approval. Landis liked the idea so much he planned to make it an annual game, with the proceeds going to the Players' Pension Fund, created to help needy former players. The All-Star Game proved such a success that it has been played for every year since, except the final war year of 1945.

The first game, played on July 6, 1933, at Comiskey Park, was won most appropriately on a home run hit by the aging Babe Ruth. That victory began nearly two decades of American League dominance, with junior circuit sluggers such as Lou Gehrig, Jimmy Foxx, Hank Greenberg, Joe

The very first National League All-Star team in 1933.

Aerial view of the 1935 All-Star Game.

DiMaggio and Ted Williams generally proving too potent for the National League. When the American League took the 1949 game by an 11-7 score, it marked the twelfth victory in sixteen games. Fans wondered if the National League would ever be able to close the gap.

Yet beginning with a dramatic win in 1950, the National League began to come on, dominating the midsummer classic since then. The Nationals have turned a 4-12 deficit into a 37-20-1 advantage through 1987. Which means that the senior circuit has won 33 games and lost only 8 since 1950, an incredible .805 winning percentage. Certainly, the World Series, the only other fully competitive game in which the two leagues meet, has not seen that kind of one-league dominance. There has been a brace of theories as to why the Nationals dominate the All-Star Game—from the National League jumping the gun by signing the top black players after Jackie Robinson broke the color line in 1947, to the Nationals just want to win more. Whatever the reason, there is no denying the facts. It's been a National League game since 1950.

Meanwhile, the selection process underwent some changes. In 1935, rival managers picked the players. That lasted until 1938 when it was decided that the eight managers in each league could best fill the rosters. And in 1947, it changed again. Once again, the fans were allowed to select the teams by a nationwide ballot. After ten years of fan selection, things got out of control. The 1957 team had seven players on it from Cincinnati. The Cincinnati fans were stuffing the ballot boxes with pre-printed ballots found in the newspaper. Baseball Commissioner Ford C. Frick had seen enough. The following year, the vote was given to the managers, coaches and players.

It remained like that until 1970. At that time, Bowie

Kuhn felt that the selection should be returned to the fans. It has been that way every since.

Great All-Star Games will look at some of the best games during the nearly forty years that the National League has dominated the midsummer classic—the heroes and the goats, the great plays and outstanding individual performances that have made the difference between winning and losing. The game is more popular than ever. A full house has become the norm, and in recent years the prime-time television audience has numbered in the tens of millions. In many ways, the All-Star Game is everything Arch Ward thought it would be. And now it's time to play ball!

Memories of Babe Ruth ran deep whenever someone hit an All-Star home run. The Babe hit the first one in 1933.

The 1950 Game

It was the start of a new decade, and as the Philadelphia Phillies "Whiz Kids" moved inexorably toward an October date with the ever-powerful New York Yankees, the All-Stars gathered once again at Comiskey Park in Chicago, where the whole thing had started seventeen years before. The date was July 11, and the American Leaguers under Casey Stengel looked to make it five straight victories over Burt Shotton's National League squad.

In the sixteen preceding seasons, the midsummer classic had made a complete tour of all sixteen big league parks, so the return to Comiskey was, in a sense, a new beginning. The Americans didn't see it that way, though. They came in

Detroit's George Kell joined Phil Rizzuto, Bobby Doerr, and Walt Dropo in the infield.

with the usual cast of talented characters. Shortstop Phil Rizzuto was en route to an MVP season with the Yanks. He was joined in the infield by George Kell of Detroit of third, Bobby Doerr of the Red Sox at second, and rookie Walt Dropo of the Bosox at first. Dropo was in the midst of a Rookie of the Year season that would see him drive in 144 runs.

The outfield had Larry Doby of the Indians, the first black in the American League back in 1947, the one and only Ted Williams, and Hoot Evers of the Tigers. Yogi Berra of the Yanks was behind the plate. It was a year in which both Joe and Dom DiMaggio were among the reserves. That's the kind of team the American League had, the same type that had

Two birds—Marty Marion and Red Schoendienst.

helped build the 12-4 advantage. Throw in the likes of Vic Raschi and Allie Reynolds of the Yanks, Bob Lemon and Bob Feller of the Indians, and there was a quartet of great pitchers right there.

While the American Leaguers might have been the favorites, the National League was bringing in a solid club. The team had good power with the likes of Ralph Kiner of the Pirates, the great Stan Musial of the Cards, Hank Sauer of the Cubs, and Roy Campanella of the Dodgers. Throw in Jackie Robinson of the Dodgers, who was hitting .365 at the break, Marty Marion of the Cardinals, Red Schoendienst who was also from St. Louis and Andy Pafko of the Cubs, and the senior circuit had come in with a pretty good club of its own. Robin Roberts of the Phils, Don Newcombe of the Dodgers, Ewell "The Whip" Blackwell of the Reds, Jim Konstanty of the Phils, and Larry Jansen of the Giants were all top pitchers in the midst of fine seasons.

On paper, this National League aggregation could easily compete with the American Leaguers. But was there some kind of mystique that kept the American League winning? The likes of Ruth, Gehrig, Foxx, Greenberg and Simmons were gone, but it still seemed to be the American League that usually got the clutch hits, came up with the key rallies, and finished up with the win.

A minor pregame incident indicated the tremendous respect the Nationals had for the American Leaguers. Ralph Kiner, who had been the National League home-run champ ever since his rookie year of 1946, and a man who had blasted 54 round trippers just a year earlier, seemed a bit taken by the distant dimensions of Comiskey. After parking a couple in the left field seats during batting practice, Kiner said:

"Gee, they tell me that [Jimmie] Foxx hit one on the roof here. That's a real wallop."

Old Double X, of course, was one of the sluggers who helped the American League in the early days of the All-Star Game. And, indeed, he had hit four on the roof. Kiner, as powerful a hitter as anyone in the game in 1950, still seemed awed by the old American Leaguers' strength.

To make matters worse, the National League came into the 1950 game with a bit of controversy. The fans, who voted for the starting line-ups, had named a National League outfield of Ralph Kiner, Hank Sauer, and Enos Slaughter. None of them was a center fielder. Kiner played left, Slaughter right, and Sauer both left and right. Manager Burt Shotton of the Dodgers pondered his problem, then thought of a solution. He wanted to install his own fine center fielder, Duke Snider, into the starting line-up in place of Sauer, who could then come into the game as a reserve. To Shotton, it seemed the most logical way to get the strongest team onto the field.

But Baseball Commissioner A. B. "Happy" Chandler vetoed the move. He said the manager had no right to change the starting line-up, or go against the wishes of the fans. Taking it as a personal affront, the 46,000 fans at the ballpark booed Shotton unmercilessly during the pregame introductions.

"I wonder whether those 46,000 people who booed me aren't ashamed of themselves for the way they acted," the veteran skipper said later. "I stood there long enough so they could all see me. I wanted to get all the boos they had. I feel all right now, but I'm wondering how they feel."

Though thwarted in his attempt to get a natural center fielder into the line-up, Shotton still wasn't through making moves. Instead of starting Sauer in center, he moved Enos Slaughter into the middle and put the slow-footed Sauer in right. At least he'd have some speed out there, even though the

Pittsburgh slugger Ralph Kiner tied the game with a big home run in the ninth inning.

Old Double X Jimmie Foxx flanked by Averill, Gehrig, Goslin, and Higgins—the old American Leaguers still had an impact on the young Nationals.

hustling Slaughter rarely played center. But it was a move that would soon pay dividends.

Vic Raschi started against Robin Roberts, both pitchers on their way to 20-win seasons. With just one out in the top of the first, Kiner came up and pasted a Raschi fastball to deep left. Ted Williams, never known for his glove, raced back and made a great running catch a split second before hitting the wall. The Splendid Splinter held the ball, but came away clutching his left elbow. Ted rubbed it for a few minutes and then indicated that he could continue. Williams would remain in the game for eight innings, getting a hit in four trips, but the pain in his elbow kept getting worse. It was after the game that the Splinter learned the elbow was fractured and that he would need surgery. He was lost to the Red Sox until mid-September, something many feel cost the club the American League pennant.

But when it happened it was viewed simply as a great catch and more proof that the American League could do no wrong. Yet in the second inning the Nationals broke through for a pair of runs on a single by Robinson, a triple by Slaughter, and a run-scoring fly ball by Sauer. Then, in the bottom half of the inning, the Burt Shotton shuffle was vindicated.

Big Walt Dropo tagged one off Roberts that appeared headed for the center field seats. But Enos Slaughter, a never-say-die player if there ever was one, raced back and made an over-the-head-catch right in front of the bullpen to save at least a triple. It was a ball the lumbering Sauer never could have reached had he been the center fielder that day.

But the American League managed to get one back in the third when pinch hitter Cass Michaels doubled, was bunted to third by Rizzuto, and scored on a fly ball off the bat of George Kell. And while Bob Lemon had replaced Raschi

Robin Roberts—on his way to a 20-win season.

An unexpected by-product of the 1950 game was a fractured elbow suffered by the great Ted Williams. Some say the injury cost the Red Sox the pennant.

and was holding the Nationals at bay, the American League took the lead off Don Newcombe in the fifth.

Newcombe committed a major baseball sin by walking opposing pitcher Lemon to open the inning. Larry Doby then doubled off Robinson's glove, sending Lemon to third. Kell lofted another fly ball for a run as Lemon tagged and scored. Williams, still in the game despite the pain in his elbow, then singled home Doby with the second run, putting the American League up, 3-2.

Lemon pitched through the sixth, holding the National Leaguers to just a single hit in his three-inning stint. Manager Stengel then brought in Detroit's Art Houtteman, who would be a 19-game winner in 1950. Houtteman took up where Lemon left off and began setting the Nationals down.

In the sixth, Shotton had called on the Phils' Jim Konstanty, who would be in the National League's Most Valuable Player that year by appearing in 74 games and winning 16. Konstanty pitched a scoreless frame and then gave way to Larry Jansen, who would be perhaps the most brilliant hurler of the day. The Americans couldn't touch him.

The problem was that the Nationals still trailed by one run and now it was the ninth inning, Houtteman still pitching. Ralph Kiner was first up and he promptly showed that he was no longer awed by the size of the park or by ghosts of American Leaguers past. Kiner promptly poled a long homer to left. One swing of the bat and the game was tied, but more importantly, the National League now had a new lease on life and a chance to break its losing streak.

When the American League couldn't score off Jansen (who had retired nine in a row) in the ninth, the game became the first extra-inning encounter in All-Star history. Jansen pitched through the eleventh, giving up only a single to Doby

Never-say-die Enos Slaughter after he had been traded to New York.

Joe DiMaggio was among the reserves in 1950.

Ewell "The Whip" Blackwell of the Reds fired his sidearm whip successfully at the American League hitters.

in five innings, while fanning six. Right-hander Ewell Blackwell then took over, firing his sidearm whip to the American League hitters and pitching nearly as well as Jansen.

Meanwhile Yankee fireballer Allie Reynolds was tossing blanks at the Nationals for three innings through the twelfth. Detroit southpaw Ted Gray took over in the thirteenth and got the side out. But when the Nationals came up in the fourteenth, lightning struck.

It was in the form of the Cardinals' Red Schoendienst, who had entered the game for starter Jackie Robinson in the eleventh. The switch-hitting redhead picked out a Gray offering and drove it into the left field seats as American League fans fell silent. The Nationals had taken a 4-3 lead. But the American League still had one more shot at Blackwell.

The Americans managed to get a runner on first via a Ferris Fain single and with just one out the great Joe DiMaggio was up. What a time for another miracle finish for the American League. But this time it wasn't to be. DiMag smashed a Blackwell fastball on the ground to Willie Jones at third and it was turned into a bang-bang double play that ended the game. Just like that. The American League win streak was over.

Some postscripts: DiMaggio had pulled an abdominal muscle while hitting into the game-ending double play, an event, which coupled with the Williams injury, threatened to put the American League's two top stars out of action. Only Williams', however, turned out to be serious.

National Leaguers near him on the bench said that Red Schoendienst had called his shot before his dramatic, game-winning homer. The redhead was quoted as saying, "I'm gonna hit one in the seats."

Yankee coach Bill Dickey felt the game could have

gone either way. "We could have won it with a break or two," he said. "But the crowd saw a good show and I know I saw some good pitching. Reynolds and Lemon were great and so was that Jansen. And Blackwell wasn't bad at all, not at all."

But in the end, perhaps it was Casey Stengel who best summed up the 1950 All-Star Game when, in his own inimitable way, he said:

"They won it. A home run tied it and a home run won it. You can't catch them when they hit them into the seats. We don't lose easily. They had to play that hard to beat us."

The 1952 Game

With a win finally under their belts, the new-look National Leaguers came back the next year and won again, this time by a comfortable 8-3 count. Two in a row. Maybe the tide was turning. The American League didn't think so and planned to get back to winning ways at the 1952 game, scheduled for old Shibe Park in Philadelphia on July 8. Philly was scheduled to play host the year before, but deferred to Detroit so the game could be part of the Motor City's 250th anniversary celebration.

That gave Philadelphia the game in 1952 and the players and coaches gathered in the City of Brotherly Love. Piloting the National League was the fiery Leo Durocher, whose Giants had won the National League pennant in 1951 after pulling off the Little Miracle at Coogan's Bluff, coming from way behind to catch the Dodgers and win in a Bobby Thomson play-off spectacular. The American League turned once again to Casey Stengel, whose Yankees were in the midst of a five-year run as American League and world champs. And ol' Case was ready to lead his team back to winning ways.

"I got a club out there now that will win this ball game," the Professor said. "I also have a couple of guys who can hit home runs on the bench and they'll be in there as soon as we get the men on base."

There was one thing wrong with Case's game plan. It was raining. In fact, it had rained all morning and the rains were predicted to keep up intermittently all afternoon. There had never been a rainout in All-Star annals and because of the tightness of the schedule, it was decided to try to get the game in.

Roy Campanella tagging out Ferris Fain in the second inning of the 1951 All-Star Game.

Jackie Robinson was perhaps the most exciting baserunner of his time. But that didn't stop Shantz from making Robby another strikeout victim in the fifth.

Neither team took batting or infield practice prior to the game. In fact, the start was delayed for some twenty minutes by still another shower, and the more than 32,000 fans in attendance must have wondered whether or not they were going to see any baseball or not. But things finally got underway with the Yanks' Vic Raschi going up against Curt Simmons of the Phillies.

With Joe DiMaggio having retired the year before and Ted Williams recalled to military duty in Korea, the American League was missing its two great stars of the 1940s. But the junior circuit still had the likes of Dom DiMaggio, Larry Doby, Hank Bauer, Dale Mitchell, Al Rosen, Eddie Robinson, Bobby Avila, Yogi Berra and Phil Rizzuto. Still, to some the American League didn't seem quite as formidable as in the recent past.

The Nationals, with the likes of Whitey Lockman, Jackie Robinson, Stan Musial, Hank Sauer, Roy Campanella, Enos Slaughter, Bobby Thomson and Granny Hamner seemed to match up well offensively. Perhaps it was going to be a game that came down to pitching...and the weather.

Right-hander Raschi must have been plenty familiar to the National Leaguers by then. The Springfield Rifle, as he was called, was working in his fourth All-Star Game in five years. Jackie Robinson, at least, was ready for him. For with just one out in the bottom of the first, Robby pickled one and sent it through the raindrops deep into the upper left field stands, giving the Nationals a 1-0 lead. Simmons, meanwhile, was using his herky-jerky windup and stylish southpaw slants to stymie the American League hitters. The former Whiz Kid, returning from a stint in the service, worked three scoreless innings giving up a single hit and striking out three.

But when Simmons gave way to Cubs' righty Bob Rush

in the fourth, the American League came to life. Minnie Minoso of the White Sox greeted Rush with a double. Then Cleveland's Al Rosen walked. After Yogi Berra went out, Eddie Robinson of the White Sox hit a shot off Jackie Robinson's glove at second. The base hit scored Minoso and sent Rosen steaming into third.

When Bobby Avila beat out an infield hit to score Rosen and give the Americans a 2-1 lead, it looked as if a big inning might be in the works. Phil Rizzuto was next and the Scooter promptly hit a grounder to Granny Hamner at short. But, as he tried to leave the batter's box the usually quick Rizzuto slipped on the wet ground and fell, making him an easy double play victim at first and ending the inning.

The rain continued to fall and playing conditions worsened. Instead of using a brush to clean off home plate, the umpire was now using a towel. The question now on everyone's minds was just how long it could go on this way. But the Nationals nevertheless came up in the bottom of the fourth to face the Indians' Bob Lemon, who had come on for Raschi the inning before. The crafty right-hander retired Robinson to open the inning, and now Musial was up.

Lemon checked out The Man and his peek-a-boo stance—and promptly hit him with a pitch. That brought up big Sauer, who had been the center of that fielding controversy just two years earlier. This time around the big guy was en route to a season that would see him club 37 homers and drive home 121 runs. Both figures would lead the league and earn Sauer an MVP prize. He didn't disappoint in the All-Star Game, either. Going after Lemon's first pitch, he hit a long shot onto the left field roof for a home run. The Nationals had gone in front, 3-2.

With new-found confidence, the National Leaguers

looked to break it open. After Sauer's home run, Lemon walked Campanella, then gave up a double to hustling Enos Slaughter. With runners on second and third, however, Bobby Thomson fouled out to third. An intentional walk to Granny Hamner loaded the bases, and perhaps surprisingly, Durocher let Rush bat for himself. The pitcher grounded out to Rosen.

But the Nationals had the lead and Rush quickly retired the Americans in the top of the fifth. Then, with weather conditions worsening, Casey Stengel called upon the Philadelphia A's little left-hander, Bobby Shantz. The 5'6", 140-pounder was in the midst of the career season, one that would see him finish with a 24-7 record and become the league's Most Valuable Player.

As Shantz walked in from the bullpen the fans at Shibe Park roared, just as they had roared for the Phils' Curt

Bobby Shantz of the A's was a ray of sunshine on a rainy Philadelphia day in 1952 when he fanned three straight National Leaguers.

21

Giant's first baseman Whitey Lockman was Shantz' first strikeout victim of the fifth inning.

Simmons at the start of the game. Both the A's and Phils shared the old ballpark then, so it didn't take much for allegiances to change. And Bobby Shantz was about to give them something to really roar about.

Showing a surprising fastball for a pitcher his size, Shantz went to work and struck out the Giants' Whitey Lockman. Next came Jackie Robinson, never an easy hitter to fan. But Shantz whiffed him as well. Now the crowd was really yelling as none other than Stan Musial stepped up. But Shantz went to work again and seconds later The Man was leaving home plate, the third straight victim of Bobby Shantz's strikeout magic.

It didn't take much to figure out what all the buzzing was about in the press box. Shantz' three straight strikeouts now put him within reach of a legendary All-Star Game record. Back in 1934, King Carl Hubbell of the Giants had fanned five consecutive American League hitters. And what a five they were! Hall of Famers Babe Ruth, Lou Gehrig, Jimmie Foxx, Al Simmons, and Joe Cronin. Shantz wasn't facing hitters of quite the same magnitude perhaps, but Musial and Robinson were close, and Lockman wasn't exactly chopped liver, either. Would he get two or more to tie the record? Or maybe three more to break it? Unfortunately, it was a question that would never be answered. Before the sixth inning could begin, the umpires decided they had seen enough. The field was becoming increasingly unplayable. They called time. Players and fans sweated it out for nearly an hour, but the rain wouldn't stop. So after a fifty-six minute delay, the game was officially called and the National Leaguers had themselves a third straight victory. As for Bobby Shantz, he was left

In 1934, King Carl Hubbell of the Giants fanned a record five consecutive American League hitters. He is the second to last on the right—flanked by Van Lingle Mungo, Dizzy Dean, Lon Warneke, and Curt Davis.

thinking about what might have been, and he took it out on American League hitters for the rest of the year.

So in three short years a 12-4 margin had narrowed to 12-7. Was it a trend, or just the law of averages speaking its piece? Hard to say. It would take more time and more All-Star games to find out. But one respected writer, Arthur Daley of the *New York Times,* was one who thought that times were changing. Following the game, Daley wrote, in part:

"Once upon a time the American Leaguers held all the patents on winning. They just turned loose a strong-backed group of window-breakers and let them blast away. But, the patent apparently has fallen into the public domain or else the Nationals brazenly stole away the idea. For the third straight year they have succeeded by hammering out more home runs than their junior rivals."

The tide, it seemed, was a-turnin'.

The 1955 Game

The 1955 All-Star Game began on a sad note. Arch Ward had just died three days earlier in Chicago. The man who had started the whole thing was being laid to rest on the day of the game, and baseball saw fit to pay tribute to him before the action began on July 15, at Milwaukee's County Stadium, where more than 45,000 fans jammed the park to witness the city's first star-studded tilt. The Braves had moved from Boston to Milwaukee only two years earlier, so hosting the All-Star Game was a festive occasion.

On the field, the American League was hoping the momentum was with them. The Nationals had won again in 1953, making it four straight, but the junior circuit had

On his way to an American League batting title at the age of twenty, young Al Kaline made his first All-Star appearance in 1955.

bounced back to win the next one in vintage American League style, coming out on top of an 11-9 slugfest. But a close look at the star-filled rosters in 1955 showed a number of new and exciting faces, plus some indications that the balance of power might be shifting.

The American League had such exciting young players as slugger Mickey Mantle of the Yanks, the heir apparent in the Bomber superstar line of Ruth, Gehrig, and DiMaggio. Detroit sent shortstop Harvey Kuenn, who had been Rookie of the Year in 1953, a twenty year-old phenom named Al Kaline, who was only leading the league in hitting. There were also old hands like Ted Williams, Nellie Fox, Mickey Vernon, Al Rosen and Bobby Avila.

For the Nationals there were veteran stars such as Stan Musial, Duke Snider, Del Ennis, and Red Schoendienst, plus some veterans who had finally achieved star status. These players included the likes of Ted Kluszewski of the Reds, Don Mueller of the Giants, Johnny Logan and Del Crandall of the Braves, and Randy Jackson of the Cubs.

And then there were the youngsters. This was the area in which the National League was beginning to attract some real attention. They had some great young players. Appearing in the 1955 game were the likes of Braves' third baseman Eddie Mathews, who had blasted 47 homers in 1953, his second season in the league; and shortstop Ernie Banks of the Cubs, only in his third season but en route to a 44-homer campaign.

Then there was wondrous Willie Mays. The "Say Hey" Kid had been brought up by the Giants early in the 1951 season, then spent two years in the service. Returning in 1954, he blasted 41 home runs, drove in 110 runs, led the league in hitting at .345 and was the National League MVP. He was

Young superstars Mickey Mantle (left) and Willie Mays would appear in many All-Star tilts. The Mick was good, but the Say Hey Kid would sparkle nearly every year.

already being called the most exciting player of his generation and would make the All-Star Game a personal stage for his heroics over the next decade and a half.

And then there was Henry Aaron of the Braves. In just his second season, the young outfielder was already showing people what a fine all-around player he was becoming. And would continue to become.

With all these players capable of hitting the ball out, the National League was beginning to take some of the powerhitting thunder away from the junior circuit, which had boasted the big bats for so long. In fact, coming into the 1955 game, Kluszewski already had 29 home runs, Snider 28, Mays 27, Banks 23, and Mathews 22. The American League, indeed, had something to fear.

The starting pitchers were left-hander Billy Pierce for the American League and righty Robin Roberts for the Nationals. Roberts, in fact, was starting his fifth All-Star Game in six years and the American League was starting to get to him. A year earlier Roberts had given up four runs during his three-inning stint, and he got off to an even rockier start this time.

Singles by Kuenn and Fox started things off, and before the National League crowd could settle in its seats, the Americans had runners at the corners and no one out. With Ted Williams up, Roberts uncorked a wild pitch, allowing Kuenn to score. Then Williams walked and young Mickey Mantle stepped in.

The most powerful switch hitter in baseball history wasn't yet twenty-four years old, but he could poke it as far as anyone. Batting left-handed, the Mick caught a Roberts fastball and sent it well beyond the center field fence for a three-run homer that gave the Americans a 4-0 lead before a single batter had been retired. Roberts took a deep breath and, to his credit as a competitor, got the side out. He then completed his three-inning stint without further damage.

But the four-run lead looked like a comfortable cushion for awhile as Billy Pierce breezed through his three innings in awesome style, giving up a single hit while striking out three.

"I didn't know he was so fast," Manager Durocher said of Pierce. "He really had something today, the kind of stuff nobody was gonna hit much."

The next question was, could the Nationals hit Early Wynn? The burly right-hander of the Cleveland Indians had won 23 games in the pennant year of 1954, and was one of the game's top competitors. On this particular day he was nearly as good as Pierce, giving up just three hits during three innings of work.

Meanwhile, the Americans couldn't really touch Roberts' successor, lefty Harvey Haddix, in the fourth or fifth. But in the sixth they got to him for a run. It came about on a single by Berra, a double by the youngster Kaline, and a ground out. It was good enough to give the junior circuit a commanding 5-0 lead and with Yankee ace Whitey Ford warming up in the bullpen, that lead looked mighty good.

But before Ford took the hill the Americans batted against Don Newcombe in the top of the seventh. Big Newk gave up a single to Chico Carrasquel and with two out up stepped Ted Williams. The Splinter tagged one deep to right center. Running out from under this cap, Willie Mays raced to the wall and made a sensational, leaping catch, robbing Williams of a two-run homer. But the lead was still 5-0 as Whitey Ford ambled in from the bullpen.

Ford had joined the Yanks midway through the 1950 campaign and the crafty southpaw helped pitch the Bombers

The Nationals treated Whitey Ford like an Edsel during his 1955 appearance.

to a pennant that year with an impressive 9-1 record. Then, after two years in the service, Ford came back as effective as ever, compiling an 18-6 mark in his first full season of 1953. Now his job was to try to keep the National League sluggers at bay.

Ted Kluszewski hit a seeing-eyed Texas Leaguer in the eighth.

Maybe the Nationals forgot to read his press clippings, because on this day they treated Ford like an Edsel. Mays started with a single, and after the left-hander retired the next two hitters, Hank Aaron walked. Then Johnny Logan delighted the home crowd by singling Mays home. An error by shortstop Carrasquel on a Stan Lopata grounder enabled the second run to score before Ford got out of the jam.

But if he got out of the jam in the seventh, he was right back in the soup in the eighth. And this time it didn't start until two were out. Mays and Kluszewski singled, Big Klu's being a seeing-eyed Texas Leaguer that fell just beyond the infield. A run-scoring base hit by Randy Jackson sent Ford to the showers in favor of Boston right-hander Frank Sullivan. Sullivan was greeted by Hank Aaron's RBI base hit to right. Kaline charged the ball and tried to nail Jackson at third, but the throw skipped away from Rosen, enabling Jackson to continue to the plate with the tying run. It was an inning the American League would remember and regret.

With the score at 5-5, the game suddenly turned into a pitchers' battle. Sullivan settled down and began mowing down the seniors, while Cincy's Joe Nuxhall was doing the same to the American Leaguers. Nuxhall had bailed the Nationals out of a bases-loaded jam in the eighth and was equally impressive in the ninth. Often remembered for his appearance as a fifteen year old in 1945, Nuxhall returned to the Bigs in 1952 and became a solid pitcher. Now he helped move the 1955 All-Star Game into extra innings.

The Americans mounted a threat in the eleventh when they put runners on first and second with two out. Then Nuxhall had to face the ever-dangerous Yogi Berra, one of the toughest clutch hitters in the game. Yog bounced one over the mound that seemed center field-bound until Red Schoendienst made a lunging, backhanded grab and equally tough off-balance throw to first, nailing Berra by a step and possibly saving the game.

Now the contest went into the twelfth. The hometown fans roared once more as the Braves' Gene Conley took the mound. Conley was a 6'8" right-hander who spent his spare time playing backup center for the Boston Celtics. And he struck a note for all two-sport stars when he promptly fanned Kaline, Mickey Vernon, and Al Rosen in rapid succession. The fans roared some more.

Frank Sullivan was in his fourth inning of work when Stan Musial got ready to lead off the twelfth. As The Man left the dugout, Coach Harry Walker yelled to him:

"Let's end this thing now, Stan. I'm getting hungry."

Though Musial probably wasn't worried about Walker's appetite, he was one of baseball's best hitters. And when

As Stan The Man left the dugout to lead off in the twelfth, Coach Harry Walker told him to finish the game already...

...and he didn't disappoint. He whacked the ball into the seats for the game-winning home run.

Sullivan started him off with a juicy fastball, Stan sprung out of his crouch and whacked the ball deep into the seats for agame-winning home run. The Nationals had done it again, 6-5.

"I never even looked back," said a disconsolate Sullivan. "As soon as he hit it, I knew that was that."

Musial agreed. "I knew it was gone when I hit it," The Man said.

Manager Lopez saw the turning point back in the eighth. "That blooper Kluszewski hit was the turning point," the skipper said.

Hey, but what if Mays hadn't caught Williams' long drive in the seventh? You could "what if" it to death, but there was one undeniable fact. It was now the National League that was finding new ways to win the All-Star Game, and that was something that had belonged exclusively to the American League for so long. But apparently they no longer had the market cornered when it came to last-minute baseball magic.

The 1959 & 1960 Games

While the American League had gained a small measure of revenge by winning two of the next three games, both leagues approached All-Star time in 1959 with curiosity and some trepidation. For the people who ran the game were about to try a radical new idea. Instead of a single All-Star Game, beginning in 1959 there would be two. That way, more people could see the stars perform, revenue would be doubled, and the game would get some added exposure.

The first of the 1959 games was set for July 7, at Forbes Field in Pittsburgh, while the second would be played nearly a month later on August 7, at the Los Angeles Coliseum. The Coliseum was the temporary home of the Los Angeles Dodgers, the transplanted Brooklyn franchise that had moved to the West Coast in 1958, at the same time the New York Giants moved to San Francisco.

Reaction to the second All-Star Game was mixed, but everyone figured they'd try it on for size. The first game saw Don Drysdale of the Dodgers starting against veteran Early Wynn, who was now pitching for the White Sox. For six innings it was a mound duel. Wynn was touched for a first-inning homer by Eddie Mathews, while Drysdale retired nine straight in his three-inning sting. Catcher Del Crandall of the Braves worked behind the plate during Drysdale's turn and was impressed.

"I always suspected I was overmatched when I stepped up against Don," Crandall said. "Now, after catching him, I'm sure of it."

Next came Yanks' reliever Ryne Duren and Lew Burdette of the Braves. The only run off this pair was an Al Kaline homer in the fourth. So after six the game was tied at one. Then it got interesting.

After the Pirates' Elroy Face—in the midst of an incredible 18-1 season—retired the American League hitters in the seventh, the Nationals went to work on Jim Bunning of the Tigers. Ernie Banks started things with a solid double. Then after two were out, Del Crandall rapped a single to score Banks with the tie-breaking run. The alert Crandall had taken second on the throw home, and moments later scored on a base hit by the Pirates Bill Mazeroski. That made it 3-1, but the two-run rally also seemed to wake up the American League bats against Face in the eighth.

Using his forkball, Face retired the first two American League hitters and seemed ready to breeze through another inning. But a Nellie Fox single, followed by a walk to Harvey Kuenn, set things up for the Indians' Vic Power, who whacked a run-scoring single. With slugger Rocky Colavito due up, Manager Stengel called him back and sent up the aging Ted Williams, who was not having a good year, but who was always a dangerous hitter. ("If I have to be pinch hit for, I'm glad it's by Ted Williams," Colavito would say later. "He's the best.") Face was being careful, too, because he walked the veteran slugger, filling the sacks.

Now Baltimore catcher Gus Triandos was up. Digging in, Triandos slammed a double to score the tying and go-ahead runs. Manager Fred Haney called for lefty John Antonelli, who came on and got the final out. But the American League had taken the lead, 4-3. And when the Nationals came up in the bottom of the eighth they were facing Yankee ace Whitey Ford.

The Cards' Ken Boyer greeted the southpaw with a base

All-Star pitchers would have preferred seeing Willie Mays this way. Standing up, he wore out the American League in both 1959 and 1960.

hit and was promptly sacrificed to second. Hank Aaron was next, and the Braves' star slammed another single to score Boyer with the tying run. Now, Willie Mays was up. The Say Hey Kid was a perfect 3-for-3 against Ford in All-Star competition and he wasn't about to break the string. This time he slammed a long triple to right center field, scoring Aaron, sending Ford to the showers, and the team into the lead, 5-4.

"I never have gotten him out," Ford lamented later. "He hits me like he owns me."

Mays deadpanned his game-winning hit. "Yeah, I hit it pretty good," he said. "It was a fastball, low and away."

And that was the winning of it. Don Elston of the Cubs retired the Americans in the ninth and it was over. But this time, there was still a second game to play. And nearly a month later the two teams gathered at the mammoth Los

Angeles Coliseum, a track and football stadium converted for baseball...and not converted very well. You could hit a homer to left with a pea shooter and only fly out to right with a cannon, so out of synch were the dimensions. But the league was showcasing the sport to the City of Angels, so the Coliseum it was.

Jerry Walker of the Orioles and hometown star Don Drysdale were the starters, and to the surprise of nearly everyone, the Americans jumped on Drysdale. Manager Stengel loaded his line-up with left-handers and after the Nationals had scored a run in the first on a sacrifice fly. But the junior circuit tied it in the second when the Red Sox' Frank Malzone hit one over the short screen in left. Then in the third, Nellie Fox singled and Yogi Berra blasted his first All-Star home run to make it 3-1 in favor of the Americans.

The Nationals battled back when another of the league's young stars, Frank Robinson, belted a fifth-inning homer off veteran Early Wynn. That made it 3-2. Both ballclubs exchanged runs in the seventh, making it 4-3, before Rocky Colavito gave the American League an insurance tally with a home run off Elroy Face in the eighth. Cal McLish of Cleveland made the lead stand up with a pair of scoreless innings and the Americans had won the second game of 1959, making the year's play a standoff.

After the game, Yogi Berra said the Yanks had voted for the two games because "It was for a good cause." But he added quickly, "If they do it again, I'd like to see them played within five days."

On the other side of the coin was Baltimore manager Paul Richards, who simply called the two games "a travesty."

But both managers wanted to win. In the first game, Fred Haney of the Nationals had allowed six of his starters—

Aaron, Mays, Banks, Crandall, Wally Moon, and Orlando Cepeda—to go the full nine innings, and in the second contest, Casey Stengel defended his decision not to just put players in for the sake of an appearance.

"In a game like this you can't always get everybody in," Ol' Case said. "After all, I didn't get three pretty good Yankees in there, either," he added, naming Elston Howard, Ryne Duren and Bobby Richardson.

But there was something else about the second 1959 game. A look at the American League roster showed just one black player, Vic Power of the Indians. The National League side of the ledger showed eight and their names were Aaron, Mays, Banks, Robinson, all future Hall of Famers, as well as Junior Gilliam, Charlie Neal, pitcher Sam Jones and Vada

Vic Power, then with the Indians, was the only black American Leaguer in the second 1959 game. Many felt the Nationals were dominating because of the number of outstanding black players in the league.

Pinson. Many people equate the start of National League domination with the league's aggressiveness in signing good, young black stars in the years following Jackie Robinson's breaking of the color line in 1947. A look at the 1959 rosters does give some credence to that theory.

A year later there were two games once again. But, believe it or not, someone decided to take Yogi Berra's advice. Instead of spacing the games nearly a month apart, they were scheduled during one All-Star break, July 11 at Kansas City and July 13, at Yankee Stadium in New York.

Because the White Sox had broken the Yankee stranglehold on the American League pennant, Al Lopez replaced Stengel as All-Star manager and would set a mark by using all 25 of his players. But the National League line-up looked extremely powerful. Mays was hitting .353 at the break, while Ernie Banks had twenty-six homers. For the Americans, the Yanks' Roger Maris had already blasted 27.

Veteran pitcher Early Wynn thought the weather was a bit hot in 1960.

It was an extremely hot July day in Kansas City, one that brought about some playful banter among the players. Jim Lemon of Washington began riding All-Star Pete Runnels of the Red Sox.

"I feel sorry for you, Pete," Lemon said. "While you're broiling to death beneath that hot Kansas City sun, I'll be sitting beside a swimming pool, sipping a cool drink and watching you guys on television."

As fate would have it, Lemon was called upon as a last-minute replacement for teammate Camilo Pascual, who was scratched. And during the game, when Lemon came off the field drenched with perspiration, a smiling Runnels quipped, "Fancy meeting you here, Jim. Say, weren't you gonna be someplace else?"

Veteran pitcher Early Wynn was more to the point in describing the heat. "When I stepped out of the air-conditioned

The Splendid Splinter Ted Williams hit his last All-Star ball in 1960.

dressing room," Wynn said, "it was like getting hit in the face with a blowtorch."

It didn't take the Nationals long to generate some heat of their own. The Americans started Bill Monbouquette of the Red Sox, and Monbo was touched up for four runs in two innings, three of them coming in the first. Will Mays (who else?) opened things up with a triple, scored on a single by the Pirates' Bob Skinner and then cheered as Ernie Banks blasted a two-run homer to give the Nationals a fast 3-0 lead.

A Del Crandall homer made it 4-0 in the second, and in the third they got another off Chuck Estrada of Baltimore, this one coming home on a double by Banks and singles by Joe Adcock of Milwaukee and Bill Mazeroski of the Pirates. That gave the senior circuit five runs. It was all they'd get as Jim Coates, Gary Bell, Frank Lary and Bud Daley shut the door for the Americans.

But the five would be enough. The host team got one back in the sixth off Mike McCormick, an unearned tally, then got two more in the eighth, one of which was unearned. The American League threatened once more in the ninth, but with two on and one out, Vern Law of Pittsburgh came on and retired Brooks Robinson and Harvey Kuenn to end it. Pirate starter Bob Friend, who went the first three, was the winner.

The second game of 1960 was symbolic in a way. The National League won it, 6-0. It was the first shutout since 1946, which the American League had won, 12-0. But now things were reversed, and in more ways than one. With the likes of Mays, Aaron, Banks, Adcock, Mathews, Cepeda, Clemente, Musial, Boyer, and others, the senior circuit was loaded with power, and with outstanding players. Somehow, the American League line-up, in spite of the likes of Mantle, Maris and Kaline, did not quite measure up.

Whitey Ford was the starter for the junior circuit and the first batter he had to face was Willie Mays. Willie singled to keep his perfect streak against Ford intact. And while the Yankee stalwart got through the inning without further damage, he was subsequently rocked for a two-run blast by Mathews in the second. Then in the third, Mays came up again and this time he homered, giving him six hits in six All-Star at-bats against Ford, one of the best pitchers in the game.

In the seventh, Stan Musial pinch hit a home run, his sixth in All-Star competition, and the final runs scored in the ninth as Ken Boyer slammed a two-run shot. Meanwhile, Vern Law, Johnny Padres, Stan Williams, Bill Henry, and Lindy McDaniel, none of whom was considered a superstar, shut the American League down on eight harmless hits. Perhaps the most significant was a pinch single by Ted Williams in the seventh. It was the retiring Splinter's last All-Star at-bat.

But as memorable as it was, the hit couldn't help the Americans. "We never did break through, even with all our power," the Greatest Hitter of All Time said.

In the two 1960 games, the National League had produced eight home runs to just one for the Americans. The conclusion was obvious, but in a bit or irony, senior circuit slugger Joe Adcock looked at it a bit differently.

"Good pitching will stop good hitting and our league is loaded with good pitchers," Adcock said.

The National League had taken seven of the eleven games played in the 1950s, and had opened the 1960s with a sweep of the first two. That reduced the American League's advantage to just three games at 16-13, and by the looks of the 1960 rosters, the senior circuit was going to continue riding its wave of victories right into the new decade.

The 1961 Games

The year 1961 conjures up images of power, but this time the biggest bangs were coming out of the American League, especially from the Bronx. That's where Yankees Roger Maris and Mickey Mantle were making their dual run at the legendary 60-home-run record set by the one and only Babe Ruth. And not far behind the "M & M boys," as the two Yanks were called, were the likes of Baltimore's Jim Gentile, Minnesota's Harmon Killebrew, and Detroit's Rocky Colavito.

So as the players gathered at Candlestick Park in San Francisco on July 11, for the first of the two 1961 All-Star Games, American Leaguers and their fans were hoping to produce some west coast thunder that would put the junior circuit back on track. The aforementioned sluggers were all there, as were Al Kaline and Norm Cash of Detroit, and Brooks Robinson of the Orioles. It was an American League club capable of striking quickly.

But then there was Candlestick Park, the new stadium opened in 1960 to house the San Francisco Giants after their westward move. Candlestick was a ballpark of split personality. It could be warm and placid one minute, cold and foreboding the next. And it was known for the winds. Ah, yes, the winds. They would sweep in off the bay, swirl and gust, rip and pull, with the potential to really change the course of a ballgame. So the players had to wonder just which Candlestick Park they would be seeing on July 11. As it turned out, they would see both.

Before the game, American Leaguer Yogi Berra approached his longtime friend, the National's Stan Musial, and asked which way the winds blew.

Roger Maris, Yogi Berra, and Mickey Mantle. Mantle and Maris were in the midst of the dual run at Ruth's 60-home-run record and Berra was concerned about which way the winds blew in 1961.

"Out here," replied Musial, "they blow out, but they also come in. But relax, Yog, in our league left fielders come out here for the ride. They don't have to catch the ball because the wind blows it back to the shortstop."

For awhile, though, Berra must have thought Musial was telling him some kind of fairytale. For the day was hot and balmy at gametime, and many of the more than 44,000 fans who jammed the ballpark were quite uncomfortable. In fact, during the course of the ballgame, some 95 patrons would have to be given first aid as a direct result of the heat.

The American League almost didn't come in at full strength. Arriving the day before, buddies Mickey Mantle and Whitey Ford decided to get in a round of golf at one of the local courses. Mantle, who was cursed by injury for most of his great career, didn't fare much better on the links. He was hit in the head by an errant golf ball and knocked to the ground. Ford said the ball hit him about an inch above the right eye. Fortunately, he shook it off and was ready for the game.

With Casey Stengel having been fired as Yankee manager following the 1960 season (in which he won still another pennant), Paul Richards of the second-place Orioles took over the club. And for a starting pitcher he turned to none other than Whitey Ford, who had been treated quite shabbily by the Nationals in recent years. The senior circuit, with Pittsburgh's Danny Murtaugh at the helm, tabbed the great Warren Spahn to go to the hill.

It had to be a joyous first inning for Ford. Not only did he escape without allowing a run, but he actually struck out Willie Mays, the first time he had ever retired the Say Hey Kid in All-Star competition. Unfortunately, the little lefty wasn't

Killebrew, Mays, and Mantle—this All-Star trio connected for 1,769 lifetime regular season homeruns.

so lucky in the second, when he was clipped for a run on a Roberto Clemente triple and Bill White sacrifice fly. But when he pitched a scoreless third it had to go down as one of his better All-Star outings.

There was just one problem. While Ford was giving up a run on just two hits during his three-inning stint, the forty-year-old Spahn was letter-perfect, a nine-up-nine-down performance with three strikeouts despite the potentially devastating American League line-up. And when he gave way to Bob Purkey of the Reds in the fourth, the result was the same. The American League hitters could do nothing. The Nationals had scored a second run in the fourth when Mays reached second on a two-base error and came around on a ground out and sacrifice fly by Clemente.

In the sixth, the Americans finally showed some of their vaunted power when pinch hitter Harmon Killebrew caught a

Norm Cash smacked the second hit for the Americans.

Mike McCormick fastball and took it downtown. That made it a 2-1 game and while they had just a single hit, the Americans were still in it.

But pitching continued to dominate. Dick Donovan and Jim Bunning had both shut the Nationals down, and in the bottom of the eighth the Red Sox' Mike Fornieles came into the game, and so did something else. The winds suddenly began whipping in off the bay, and in the space of just a few short minutes the whole demeanor of the ballpark changed. Yet while the weather was in transition, pinch hitter George Altman belted a solo shot off Fornieles to make it a 3-1 game. Another hit and knuckleballer Hoyt Wilhelm had to come in to get the side out.

Now the American League had one at bat left as Elroy Face took to the hill, and the winds continued to blow harder. Face got the first hitter, but then Norm Cash smacked a double, only the second hit all day for the power-laden Americans. But it woke up the sleeping giant, for Al Kaline followed with a single that drove home pinch runner Nellie Fox and brought left-hander Sandy Koufax in from the bullpen. Roger Maris greeted Koufax with a base hit and with Rocky Colavito coming up, manager Murtaugh yanked his lefty in favor of Giants righty Stu Miller.

Miller was a little guy with a variety of slow-slower-slowest curves and off-speed pitches, pitches sometimes helped by Candlestick's howling wind. And the wind was really doing its thing now, dust and papers blowing all over the field. Colavito dug in, and just as Miller got ready to deliver, a nasty gust caught him and made him stop his delivery so he could keep his balance. Otherwise, he might have fallen over. The umpire had no choice but to call a balk, and the runners advanced to second and third.

Once Miller could pitch, Colavito slammed a grounder to Ken Boyer at third, who kicked the ball allowing Kaline to score with the tying run. Despite a dropped foul pop and a bad throw, Miller managed to pitch out of further trouble. When the Nationals couldn't score off Wilhelm, the game went into the tenth.

Now the wind was playing a big part in everything. With two down, Miller walked Nellie Fox and Kaline hit a grounder to third. Boyer's throw looked to be on the mark until another huge gust blew the ball into right field. Fox came all the way around to score the go-ahead run. Suddenly, the wind had blown the Americans into a 4-3 lead.

But in the bottom of the tenth, the Nationals struck back. Aaron started it with a single and went to second on a passed ball. Then Mays, continuing his All-Star magic, slammed a double to score Aaron with the tying run. Then the wind blew a Wilhelm knuckler right into Frank Robinson, putting run-

Roberto Clemente was always sending everybody home.

ners on first and second. That's when Roberto Clemente sent everyone home by whacking a sharp single to right, scoring Mays with the winning tally.

"I was going for the distance on the first pitch," Clemente said, later. "And when that didn't work, I just tried to advance the runner. With Willie on second I knew he'd get to third on a fly to right. But when Wilhelm threw that knuckleball on the right side of the plate, everything worked out perfect."

But it really wasn't perfect. The wind saw to that. There were seven errors in the game, a game that got very wild and unpredictable after the winds started. It huffed Stu Miller off the mound, puffed a throw into right field, and helped the National League to their fourth victory in the last five games.

The second game of 1961 was also affected by the

Rocky Colavito flexed American League muscle with a first inning homer at Fenway.

weather. It was played on July 31, at Fenway Park in Boston. Ted Williams, in his first year of retirement, threw out the first ball. Before the game ended, both sides probably wished they had the Splendid Splinter's bat in the line-up.

This one was a pitcher's game from start to finish. Bob Purkey, Art Mahaffey, Sandy Koufax, and Stu Miller worked for the Nationals, while Jim Bunning, Don Schwall, and Camilo Pascual toiled for the American League. There was just nine hits in the game and two runs. The Americans scored in the first when Rocky Colavito belted a long homer over the left field wall. With Fenway always known as a hitter's park, many thought Colavito's blast was only the beginning. On the contrary, it was just about the end.

After that, nothing much happened until the sixth. Schwall was pitching for the American League when, with

Shortstop Luis Aparicio's fielding gem saved the second 1961 game for the American League, even though it ended in a 1-1 tie.

Giants' reliever Stu Miller will be forever remembered for being blown off the mound at windy Candlestick Park. But the little righty also pitched brilliantly in the second game of 1961.

one out, Ed Mathews walked. Schwall, who was pitching before his home fans at Fenway, got the dangerous Mays out, but then he hit Orlando Cepeda to put runners on first and second. Eddie Kasko of the Reds was next and hit a slow bouncer to short. Instead of charging the ball, Luis Aparicio waited on it and Kasko beat the throw, loading the bases.

Now Bill White was up, and the Cards first sacker slammed one back up the middle that had two RBIs written all over it. But Aparicio raced to his left and made a brilliant stop to keep the ball from going into center field. Mathews scored the tying run, but the bases remained loaded. Schwall then got Frank Boiling to end the inning with the score still tied. Once again the pitchers took command. But, then, suddenly the rain began to fall. Stu Miller worked the seventh, eighth and ninth for the Nationals and without the wind to buffet him, the little guy was brilliant, giving up just a single hit and fanning five with his variety of slow, tantalizing pitches. But Camilo Pascual was just as good, holding the Nationals hitless for the same three innings. Then, at the end of nine, the rain really began coming down. Time was called, and a short time later, the game was cancelled, making it the only tie in All-Star history. Afterward, the talk of the American League clubhouse was Stu Miller.

"They warned me about his slow curve," said Mickey Mantle. "But I never expected a curve that slow. Shucks, I felt like I waited an hour before I swung at that one, but I was still way out front."

Slugger Roy Sievers, who fanned with two out and a man on second in the ninth, was equally impressed. "One minute it [the ball] was over the plate and the next minute it was gone. That guy is a magician."

Fellow hurler Whitey Ford enjoyed watching Miller

work. "It was a treat," said Whitey. "I noticed how he would sort of twitch his shoulder and move his head to a side before he threw each pitch. Mantle said it was the best head fake he ever saw."

The 1961 games. They were supposed to be dominated by an array of great sluggers. But instead, it was a little guy with a slow curveball. The only opponent he couldn't handle was the wind.

The 1964 Game

This was a game that both teams had to want very badly, and for good reason. Coming in, the All-Star series stood at 17-16-1 in favor of the American League. The Nationals had continued to dominate. After a split of the 1962 games, the format was returned to a single contest for 1963, which the senior circuit had won. Every National Leaguer chosen for the 1964 squad knew a victory would enable them to tie the series.

For the Americans, there was a great deal of pride at stake. A victory and they would have at least two more years to enjoy the All-Star advantage they had from the beginning. But even with a win the question remained, "for how long?"

The players gathered at brand-new Shea Stadium in New York, where the National League's expansion franchise, the Mets, had taken up residence. There would be one prominent member of the senior circuit missing. Stan Musial had retired following the 1963 season, and The Man had been one of baseball's best All-Star performers. He had twenty hits in 63 at-bats for a .317 average, including a record six home runs.

But baseball is a cyclical game. When someone leaves, someone else arrives. Certainly there would never be another quite like Musial, but the National League line-up and roster in 1964 was a bit awe-inspiring, to manager and players alike.

Walter Alston of the Dodgers was the manager, and his comment simply was, "I think I'll take this [line-up] card back to L.A. with me so that I'll remember what a batting order should look like."

Added the Cards Ken Boyer, who was once again the

Stan Musial retired at the end of the 1963 season. The Man's presence was missed in 1964.

starting third baseman: "If I had this club to manage in the regular season, I wouldn't even bother to come to the ballpark. I could manage by telephone."

What was everyone talking about? Just a line-up that seemed laden with superstars, players who could generate power and speed. Beginning with Aaron, Mays, Clemente, Bill Williams, Cepeda, Boyer, Willie Stargell, Joe Torre and Curt Flood, the National League line-up also included young stars such as Johnny Callison and Ron Hunt. The senior circuit was indeed loaded.

And as for the Americans, well, there was Mantle and Killebrew, and Brooks Robinson, as well as a number of other fine players. But somehow they just didn't seem to stack up to the Nationals. For years, people had been saying that the caliber of play in the National League had passed that of the American because the senior circuit had singed more black players sooner, and had cultivated more black talent than the

Americans. In a sense, the All-Star rosters during this period bore this out.

Mays, Aaron, Clemente, Stargell, Williams, Cepeda, Marichal, Gibson. The names of the black and Hispanic players rolled off the tongue easily. Yet in the American, so many of the top players, such as Mantle, Kaline, Maris, Killebrew, Colavito, and Cash, were white. There were certainly some fine black players in the American League and outstanding white players in the National. But if someone was looking for a reason for the change in All-Star fortunes, this one certain bears scrutiny.

But now it was gametime. Though the Yanks had been American League champs in 1963, their manager, Ralph Houk, had moved into the front office as General Manager. So Al Lopez took over the reins of the All-Stars. He chose the colorful Dean Chance of the California Angeles to start the game. Chance, en route to a brilliant 20-9 Cy Young Award season, showed the Nationals why he would pitch eleven shutouts in 1964. He blanked them for three innings, allowing just two hits.

The Nationals had gone with old hand Don Drysdale, always a tough All-Star pitcher. Big D was sharp again, though the American League did manage to pick up an unearned run in the first. It came on a base hit by Angels shortstop Jim Fregosi, a passed ball, and a run-scoring single by Killebrew. After that, Drysdale shut the door and it was a 1-0 game after three.

Then in the fourth, the National League jumped on A's right-hander John Wyatt for a pair of runs to take the lead. And they did it once again with the long ball. First it was Billy Williams of the Cubs going for the downs, then Ken Boyer of the Cards, making it 2-1 after four. They got another in the fifth off Camilo Pascual of Minnesota when Clemente singled and came home on a double by Dick Groat.

Meanwhile, Jim Bunning of the Phils, a former American League star, kept the American League scoreless through the fifth, prompting Casey Stengel to remark, "He gets 'em out in both leagues and that shows he's a good pitcher."

Bunning gave way to Chris Short, also of the Phils, in the sixth and that's when the American League got back in it. It happened quickly as Mantle and Killebrew singled, then both rode home on a big triple by Brooks Robinson. They took the lead in the seventh when Houston's Dick Farrell hit the Yanks' Elston Howard with a pitch to open the inning. Next the dangerous Rocky Colavito doubled Howard to third and he ambled home on a long fly by Jim Fregosi. So the score was tied at three.

As the Nationals came up in the bottom of the seventh

Harmon Killebrew of the Twins was one of baseball's most-feared sluggers in the 1960s.

Willie Mays. No pitcher wanted to do battle with him—he almost always won.

the American League made a pitching change. Coming in from the bullpen was Red Sox reliever Dick Radatz, a man affectionately known as "The Monster." Radatz stood 6'6" and weighed in the neighborhood of 240 pounds. In his huge hand, a baseball began to look more like a golfball. And he threw hard—very hard. In 1963 and 1964, Radatz was the most feared reliever in baseball, compiling records of 15-6 and 16-9, appearing in 66 and 79 games respectively, and striking out well over a hitter an inning.

Throwing smoke from the right side, Radatz gave the National Leaguers a taste of what his own league had been seeing for the past several years. He breezed through the seventh and eighth innings, retiring six in a row and four of them on strikes. Now, coming into the bottom of the ninth, the

Monster was three outs away from giving the Americans a 4-3 victory. But the first batter he had to face was Willie Mays.

And so the battle began, Radatz throwing high heat and the Say Hey Kid refusing to give in. Six times Radatz threw his heater and six times Mays fouled the ball off. Finally, Willie drew a walk. He had won the battle, and now his team would try to win the war.

Trying to rattle Radatz, Mays danced off first. On the second pitch to Orlando Cepeda, Willie took off and beat catcher Elston Howard's throw to second.

"I thought I could keep him close at first, make him start back to the bag," Radatz would say. "On the first pitch, he did. I thought he did on the second, too, but obviously he didn't."

Cepeda then hit a booper over Bobby Richardson's head at second. Richardson couldn't quite reach it and when he saw it drop, Mays raced to third. First baseman Joe Pepitone grabbed the baseball and fired it home. The ball took a bad hop right over Howard's head and the ever-alert Mays raced in with the tying score. The American League wouldn't win it in regulation. Now the question was, would they win it at all?

Ken Boyer was up next and Radatz got him to pop up for the first out. Then Manager Lopez ordered the Reds' Johnny Edwards walked intentionally, setting up a possible double play. With the Mets' Ron Hunt due up, a pinch hitter emerged out of the National League dugout. It was the great Henry Aaron, only a substitute in the 1964 game. Still one of the most dangerous hitters in the game, Aaron dug in against Radatz. But this time the Monster showed his greatness. He struck Aaron out and now was possibly one hitter away from sending the game into overtime.

That hitter was young Johnny Callison of the Phils.

The real hero of the 1964 game was young John Callison of the Phils, who cracked a three-run homer to cap a National League come-from-behind rally in the ninth.

Callison had entered the game as a pinch hitter in the fifth and then went to right field. The twenty-five year-old outfielder was on his way to a 31-homer, 104-RBI season, so he certainly had the credentials. Radatz went back to his fastball and Callison was ready. He drove the first pitch high and deep to right...and into the seats for a dramatic, three-run, game-winning home run. As he circled the bases with a huge smile on his face, Callison's teammates gathered at home plate to greet him. For his homer was more than just a game-winning blast. It had enabled the Nationals to tie the All-Star series at seventeen games each.

Later, when asked if he had been told about Radatz' reputation and speed, the All-Star Game's newest hero said,"No, and it's just as well. If I had, I might have been afraid of him."

But he wasn't. In fact, it was apparent that no one in the National League feared the Americans any longer. They had definitely become dominant in All-Star action and the reaction of players and league officials showed that the game meant a great deal to those in the senior circuit.

"Nice going, troops," pitcher Sandy Koufax was heard to holler as the ballclub filed into the locker room.

Mays, whose All-Star average was now a cool .392 in fifteen games, was telling anyone who'd listen that, "We're even!"

But perhaps it was National League president Warren Giles who best summed up the feelings among National Leaguers.

"It's great to be even in this series," Giles said. "There's no substitute for victory. It was a long time coming, thirty-one years."

There was one rather humorous note from the 1964 game. The New York Mets had been a National League expansion team in 1962. With a collection of has-beens, never-was and never-would be players, the Mets were league doormats, losing 120 games their first year, and 111 their second season. But in 1962, veteran Richie Ashburn had represented the Mets at the All-Star Game and gotten a base hit. The next year, veteran Duke Snider was the Mets' rep and the old Duke of Flatbush was hitless in one trip. Then in 1964, Mets second baseman Ron Hunt became the team's first elected starter. When Hunt singled his first time up, the big scoreboard at Shea Stadium flashed the following message, "The New York Mets All-Star batting average is .667."

If only the whole team had been half that good.

The 1967 Game

It might have taken the National League thirty-one years to draw even with the Americans, but it took just one year for them to take the lead, and two years to show they weren't going to relinquish it easily. The senior circuit took both the 1965 and 1966 games. And anyone questioning the relative power of the two leagues only need to look at the starting line-up in the 1965 game.

Call it a pitcher's nightmare. It read, Willie Mays (cf), Henry Aaron (rf), Willie Stargell (lf), Richie Allen (3b), Joe Torre (c), Ernie Banks (1b), Pete Rose (2b), and Maury Wills (ss). Yet the American League didn't go quietly. They lost both games by a single run, 6-5 and 2-1. So coming into 1967, many American Leaguers felt that this would be their year.

The game was played on July 11 at Anaheim Stadium, home of the California Angels, and once again the National League line-up read like a Who's Who of baseball superstars. Brock, Clemente, Aaron, Cepeda, Allen, Perez, Torre and Mazeroski. They were just the starters. In reserve were the likes of Mays, Banks, Rose, Jimmy Wynn and Rusty Staub. The pitching wasn't exactly shabby, either, with Juan Marichal, Ferguson Jenkins, Bob Gibson, Mike Cuellar, Don Drysdale and a Mets rookie named Tom Seaver.

A look at the American League roster was impressive also. With players like Brooks Robinson, Rod Carew, Tony Oliva, Harmon Killebrew, Tony Conigliaro, Carl Yastrzemski, Bill Freehan and Rico Petrocelli, it wasn't a bad group. But there was definitely a feeling that, overall, it was a notch below the Nationals, and the reserves were not as strong. Yet the 1967 game would develop into a rather unusual one, especially with all the heavy lumber that was being dragged up to home plate, inning after inning.

The starting pitchers were Marichal of the Giants and Dean Chance, who was now with the Twins. And when the two of them finished, perhaps it should have been an indication of what was to come.

Marichal, known as the Dominican Dandy, was one of the best pitchers of his time, a future Hall of Famer who would win 243 games in his career. Possessor of a high kick and a variety of deliveries, he was extremely difficult to hit, as the American Leaguers found out over the first three innings. Marichal allowed the American League batters just a single hit in three innings, striking out three in the process.

Chance, who was on his way to a second, twenty win season, fared almost as well. He just made one bad pitch, and

Dominican Dandy Juan Marichal was one of the best pitchers of his time—he would win 243 games before he was finished.

when you made a bad pitch to Richie Allen, you could kiss it good-bye. Allen caught a Chance fastball in the second inning and drove it into the seats for a 1-0 National League lead. And that's the way it stood when the two pitchers left after three innings.

Then Ferguson Jenkins and Jim McGlothlin took over. Jenkins was en route to the first of six straight, twenty win seasons with the Cubs in a career that would see him win 284 games. McGlothlin was a slightly lesser light, but on this day had his good stuff for his two innings.

Jenkins showed no mercy for the first two innings he pitched. In fact, in the fifth he faced the aging Mickey Mantle, just a year away from retirement and now a pinch hitter for the American League The Mick came up to a thunderous ovation from the big crowd, but Jenkins slipped a fastball past him for

Brooks Robinson of the Orioles (center), flanked by two of his better-known teammates, Boog Powell (left), and Frank Robinson, slammed a solo homer for the Americans in 1967.

a called third strike. In the sixth, Jenkins made his only bad pitch. It was to Brooks Robinson of the Orioles, and the slick third baseman parked it in the left field seats, tying the ballgame at 1-1.

When Jenkins departed after the six inning, he had struck out six hitters in three innings, making nine American Leaguers who had gone down on strikes in the first six frames. McGlothlin had given up one hit with a pair of strikeouts in his two innings, before Gary Peters of the White Sox took over in the sixth. One of the hitters Peter had to face in his first inning of work was Willie Mays, pinch hitting for Lou Brock. There wasn't a baseball player or fan anywhere who didn't know that the "Say Hey" Kid had owned the All-Star Game, and like Mantle, Mays came up to a huge ovation from the predominantly American League crowd.

But that didn't faze Peters. He promptly used his fine sinker and slider to set Willie up and then nail him on a called strike three. Maybe then everyone began to get the idea. In spite of the presence of so many outstanding hitters, this All-Star Game would belong to the pitchers.

Peters didn't give up a hit in his three-inning stint, striking out four batters, while Bob Gibson of the Cards, in the prime of his great Hall of Fame career, also pitched shutout ball. At the end of nine the game was still tied at 1-1 with no hint of a breakthrough. Of course, with all those power hitters, all it would take was one swing.

The string of goose eggs continued. Chris Short and Mike Cuellar worked through the twelfth for the National League, while Al Downing of the Yanks followed Peters, and then gave way to Jim "Catfish" Hunter of the A's in the eleventh. Don Drysdale took over for the National League in the thirteenth and threw two more zero frames, while Hunter

Jim "Catfish" Hunter, shown here when he was with the Yankees, pitched five tough innings in 1967 before being tagged with the loss.

continued to work for the Americans through the fourteenth. It was now the longest extra-inning game in All-Star history and everyone wondered just how long it could go before one of the big hitters caught one.

Just to show how frustrating the game was for the hitters, Roberto Clemente of the Pirates had come into the game hitting a robust .352 and on his way to another batting title. Yet the free-swinging Clemente, who was always a contact hitter, had struck out four times during the course of the game. Hits were few and far between. Going into the fifteenth inning, each club had just eight hits. And there had only been a single base on balls all game, that to Carl Yastrzemski of the Red Sox. Yaz, who was on his way to a triple crown season, also had three hits in the game, but not even that was enough to get a run across.

As the Nationals came up for the start of the fifteenth inning, Hunter was beginning his fifth inning of work. A Hall of Famer who would win over 200 ballgames, Hunter's one

It was Tony Perez of the Reds who ended the longest All-Star Game with a fifteenth inning home run off Hunter.

weakness was a tendency to throw the home run ball. And it finally came back to haunt him in the fifteenth inning.

The hitter was Tony Perez of the Reds, who had taken over for Allen at third and was hitless in one previous at-bat. Perez was the second batter in the fifteenth, coming up after Orlando Cepeda had been retired for the first out. Hunter made one just a little too good, and Perez walloped it over the left field fence for the go-ahead run. After more than three and a half hours and fourteen-and-a-half innings of play, the National League had a 2-1 lead. And coming in to try to protect that lead was a rookie named Tom Seaver.

The twenty-two year-old Seaver would win 16 games for the lowly New York Mets in 1964, giving the franchise its first taste of respectability. By the time his career ended, Seaver had more than 300 victories, 3,500 strikeouts and a sure ticket to the Hall of Fame. But in 1967, he was just a rookie facing some pretty tough American League hitters.

Seaver started off in fine fashion, quickly retiring Harmon Killebrew and Tony Conigliaro. Then Yastrzemski was up. Yaz already had three hits and Seaver didn't want to groove one.

The result was a base on balls, Yaz's second walk of the game, and the only free pass in nearly fifteen innings of pitching on both sides. With all the line-up changes, pitcher Hunter was due up next. Manager Hank Bauer of the Orioles then sent up Chicago outfielder Ken Berry to pinch hit. Bearing down and already showing poise well beyond his years, Seaver struck out Berry to end the game. The Nationals had won again!

It had been quite a game. There were just seventeen hits in the fifteen innings, but a record thirty strikeouts. The game took some three-and-three-quarters hours to complete, and represented the fifth straight National League win, the longest streak in All-Star history. It also gave the senior circuit a 20-17-1 lead in the series. And it must have made the American League players wonder just what they had to do to beat these guys.

One great player who was not part of the 1967 All-Star Game was Sandy Koufax, the great left-hander of the Los Angeles Dodgers. Koufax, who had been the most dominant pitcher in baseball since 1961, was forced to retire after the 1966 season because an arthritic left elbow threatened to turn into a permanent disability.

National League hitters never would have guessed it, though, since in his final season of 1966 Koufax was 27-9 with a 1.73 ERA, twenty-seven complete games, and 317 strike-outs.

As a spectator at the 1967 game, Koufax told reporters what the All-Star Game had meant to to him and why it was definitely something he missed. "Yes, I miss it," he said, quickly. "Don't let anybody tell you they don't mind being left off the All-Star team. Sure, everybody would like that three-day vacation. But just leave a guy off the team and he'll miss it more than he'll miss the three-day rest. I miss the excitement and the honor. But most of all, I miss the competition. So I'll be watching and feeling a little wistful about it all."

The American League, too, must have been feeling a little wistful. For once upon a time they used to win this game.

The 1968 Game

Where have all the hitters gone? The two previous All-Star Games were both won by identical 2-1 scores despite the presence of some awesome hitting talent. And in a sense, that's what made the 1968 game interesting. Would pitching continue to dominate and begin setting a precedent for future games?

To begin with, the hitters already had two strikes against them. Strike one was the site. The 1968 game was to be played at the Houston Astrodome, making it the first game played indoors and on an artificial surface. But putting the firsts aside, the Astrodome just wasn't a good place to hit baseballs. As a rule, the ball didn't carry well there and home runs were often scarce. So hitting there wouldn't be easy. Not even the National League players had seen that much of the new arena.

The second strike? Well, 1968 was rapidly developing into a total pitcher's year. In the American League, Detroit's Denny McLain was on his way to becoming baseball's first 30-game winner since 1934. American League hitters would only bang away at a .230 clip for the year with Carl Yastrzemski becoming the batting champ with an anemic .301 average.

In the National, there was some pretty slick hurling taking place as well. Bob Gibson of the Cards had become nearly unhittable. His record in 1968 would read 22-9, and some of those were tough losses, as witnessed by his incredible 1.12 ERA, league-leading 268 strikeouts and amazing 13 shutouts. Also, the Dodgers' Don Drysdale would break another long-standing record by pitching fifty-eight straight scoreless innings, a mark that would stand for twenty years until another Dodger, Orel Hershiser, set a new standard. National League hitters would only manage a collective .243 batting average for the year.

Yet there were some fine hitters once again gracing the All-Star line-ups. But by this time the game had a reputation for sometimes doing strange things to even the best stickmen. Willie Mays and Henry Aaron may be the perfect examples. The two superstars are often considered the very best of their generation, a pair of Hall of Fame players who left a legacy of records behind when they retired. Aaron, of course, became the game's all-time home run king, with Wondrous Willie the number three slugger. No one dares question either's credentials.

Don Drysdale of the Dodgers helped start the 1968 pitchers' battle with three strong innings.

Willie, of course, was always at his best in the All-Star Game, the player American League pitchers least liked to see up there. In fact, the Say Hey Kid was personally responsible for several National League victories. Aaron, on the other hand, never seemed to get untracked in the midsummer classic. His usual heroics were few and far between come All-Star time.

"Funny thing about it is that I've been plain lousy in All-Star games," Bad Henry said, trying to explain the strange phenomenon after the 1968 game. "I can't really explain it. In seventeen games I've batted .166, but my World Series average is .364. So you can't blame it on folding under pressure. Maybe I try too hard and press too much in All-Star

"There's only today," is how Henry Aaron described the pressure of the All-Star Game.

play. I'm at my best when I'm relaxed. In the World Series a guy gets a feeling there's always tomorrow. But in All-Star games there are no tomorrows. There's only today."

Interesting. If nothing else, Bad Henry was admitting that there is pressure in the All-Star Game. It isn't just a midsummer outing of fun and games where the laughs outnumber the base hits and great catches. At least that's the way it was with the National League. There are those who had maintained that the Nationals had a higher intensity level in the midsummer classic. It's possible, especially perhaps when they were chasing the Americans, who also may have become too used to winning. But once the senior circuit caught and passed their junior counterparts, the American League should have been itching to keep pace.

Now, in a pitcher's year, the two sides squared off again.

Willie McCovey of the Giants always wielded a mighty bat. But it was his double play grounder that brought home the only run of the 1968 midsummer classic.

Big Don Drysdale made a record-tying fifth start for the Nationals and was opposed by the Indians' Luis Tiant. Drysdale set the American League down with little trouble in the first and then Tiant took the mound. The lead-off hitter was none other than the aforementioned Mays, in the starting line-up because of an injury to Pete Rose. And, as usual, Willie was a catalyst.

He promptly rapped a single to left for yet another All-Star hit. Knowing Willie's propensity for running, Tiant tried a pickoff throw to first and the ball got past Harmon Killebrew for an error, Mays scooting quickly to second. Now Curt Flood was up. Tiant got behind in the count and on a pitch that was called ball four, the ball got away from catcher Jose Azcue and Mays was able to scamper to third. Then, with runners on first and third, the powerful Willie McCovey could do no better than to ground into a doubleplay. But it was enough to get Mays across with the first run of the game.

The unearned tally was one of the strangest runs in All-Star competition, but fortunately they all count the same. Because after Mays' tally, the pitchers and the Astrodome took over. Neither team was able to mount any real offense. In fact, with Drysdale, Juan Marichal, Steve Carlton, Tom Seaver, Ron Reed, and Jerry Koosman all pitching for the Nationals, the American Leaguers managed just three hits.

Meanwhile, the Nationals had only four more hits after Mays' opening single, with Blue Moon Odom, Denny McLain, Sudden Sam McDowell, Mel Stottlemyre and Tommy John all seeing hill action. Eleven American Leaguers went down on strikes, while nine Nationals fanned in another display of overpowering pitching and very little hitting.

Like Mays and Stan Musial before him, who always seemed to hit well in All-Star competition, there were also

Young Tom Seaver of the Mets was one of six National League pitchers who hurled goose eggs in the first All-Star Game at the Astrodome.

some pitchers who continually tamed the opposition. Drysdale, for instance, threw one-hit ball for three innings. It was the Big D's eighth and last All-Star Game and he left with a nineteen strikeouts in nineteen-and-one-third innings, a 1.40 ERA, and 2-1 won-lost record. Though they beat him once, all Drysdale's other appearances were dominating.

    Perhaps the most effective pitcher in the 1968 game was Met Tom Seaver. The stocky right-hander threw two innings and fanned five hitters during that time. Yet when someone asked Boston's Carl Yastrzemski to name the toughest pitcher in the game, Yaz had to think. "I don't know," he said, momentarily. "It's like asking if you want to be shot with a pistol or a shotgun. They all know what to do with the ball and in the seven years I've been with Boston they keep getting better and better."

As National League skipper Red Schoendienst added: "There's not much you can say about a 1-0 game."

It was the first 1-0 game in All-Star history. And to make the futility at the plate stand out even more, the run was unearned. At one point, twenty American League hitters were retired in succession, from the first to the seventh inning, when Tony Oliva finally doubled. And even worse for the Americans was the fact that they had scored just a single run in their last thirty-two innings of All-Star play, two in the last thirty-four, which took them back to 1966. And in those thirty-four innings, the American League had just seventeen hits and a .149 batting average. During that same span, the Nationals had only twenty hits and a .180 average. They weren't doing much better.

The game was also remembered for a couple of other things. One was the serious injury suffered by Harmon Killebrew in the third inning. The Twins' first sacker was stretching for a low throw from shortstop Jim Fregosi on a grounder hit by Curt Flood. He sustained a hamstring tear and missed nearly two months of regular season.

In addition, the game at the Astrodome was also the first All-Star Game played at night, which put it on prime-time television. The result was the sixth National League win in a row. But all those new viewers, perhaps seeing the midsummer classic for the first time, must have asked essentially the same question:

Where have all the hitters gone?

The 1970 Game

The law of averages paid a visit to the All-Stars in 1969, as the hitters got themselves a small measure of revenge, especially on the National League side of the ledger. The Nationals scored nine times the first four innings and walked away with an easy 9-3 victory, their seventh in a row. So as the 1970 game approached, there was more pressure than ever on the Americans to show they could win again.

It was beginning to seem as if the Nationals always managed to find a way to win, whether it be a low-scoring or high-scoring game. When a big hit was needed, the Nationals got it. When a game was decided on a break, it went the Nationals' way. When heroics were needed from an unlikely source, the hero always came from the senior circuit. Now the stars converged once again, this time at Cincinnati's brand-new Riverfront Stadium which, like many of the new ballparks, had an artificial surface.

Game day was July 14, and the managers were Earl Weaver for the Americans and Gil Hodges for the Nationals. The baseball world was still buzzing over the finish to the 1969 season, when Hodges and his miracle New York Mets came from ninth place in 1968 to a world championship. And one of the prime architects of that miracle, Cy Young Award winner Tom Seaver, was slated to be the National League's starting pitcher. He would be opposed by Baltimore's Jim Palmer, on the way to the first of eight 20-win seasons.

This one began as if it was a return to the punchless games of 1966-68. Both Seaver and Palmer were brilliant. Each gave up just a single hit and no runs. Seaver fanned four,

The Orioles' Jim Palmer showed the Nationals why he was a top American League hurler for more than a decade.

Palmer three, and each left with the hitters wondering what they had been seeing out there.

Things didn't change much when left-handers Sam McDowell and Jim Merritt took over. Sudden Sam, who had fanned 325 batters back in 1965, was on a 20-win, 300-strikeout course once again. Despite the presence of hitters such as Mays, Aaron, McCovey, Allen, Rose, Perez, Rico Carty, and ·Johnny Bench, the Nationals couldn't touch McDowell's heat. He duplicated Palmer's performance by allowing just a single hit and striking out three. Though he walked three, McDowell didn't really allow the Nationals to get on track.

Merritt, who threw a variety of curves and off-speed pitches for the Reds, would also win twenty in 1970. He held the Americans in check for two innings, giving them just a single hit. The junior circuit line-up in 1970 was a good one. Luis Aparicio was followed by Carl Yastrzemski, Frank Robinson, Willie Horton, Boog Powell, Amos Otis, Harmon

Carl Yastrzemski of the Red Sox had a big 1970 Game with four hits. But Yaz' heroics still couldn't guarantee the luckless American League a win.

Killebrew, Brooks Robinson, Frank Howard, Tony Oliva, Davey Johnson and Ray Fosse. The club had some heavy hitters out there.

As the Americans came out for the top of the sixth, the Nationals brought veteran Gaylord Perry to the mound. The hard-throwing right-hander was a big winner, but was often accused of throwing a slightly wet pitch among his repertoire. The Americans weren't awed, however. Catcher Ray Fosse of the Indians singled, was sacrificed to second by McDowell, and came home on an RBI single by Yaz. The American League had a 1-0 lead. Maybe this would finally be their year.

In the seventh, the junior circuit went to work again. This time Brooks Robinson singled off Perry, and Tony Oliva walked. With runners on first and second, the Orioles' Davey Johnson scratched out an infield hit to load the bases and Fosse smacked a sacrifice fly. Perry pitched out of further trouble, but the Americans now had a 2-0 lead, and the Nationals were down to their final nine outs.

In the bottom of the inning, the Americans brought Jim Perry in to pitch. Jim was Gaylord's big brother and was on his way to a 24-win season with the Twins. They were quite a pair, but what's fair for one brother was fair for the other. The Nationals got to Jim Perry quickly. And it was the bottom of the order that did the damage. The Mets' Bud Harrelson singled, followed by a walk to San Diego's Cito Gaston. Then Perry hit the Astros' Denis Menke. Suddenly the bases were loaded with none out and it looked as if the National League was going to blow the game open right then and there.

Now Perry was facing Willie McCovey, and if anyone had the potential to clear the bases with one swing it was big "Stretch." But incredibly, Perry got McCovey to ground into a doubleplay, Harrelson crossing the plate with the first National League run. Then, with the tying run just 90 feet away, Perry reached back and fanned Richie Allen to end the inning with just a single tally. So the American League still had the lead at 2-1 after seven, but the fun was just beginning.

In the top of the eighth Manager Hodges brought in Bob Gibson to hold the fort. Gibson, an incredible money pitcher who was always at his best in the World Series and would be a 23-7 pitcher in 1970, wasn't treated very well by the American Leaguers. Yastrzemski and the Tigers' Willie Horton started it off with singles, then Brooks Robinson made his second hit a good one. He slammed a triple that brought home Yaz and Horton with the third and fourth runs. Now it was a 4-1 game, and when Perry retired the Nationals in the eighth, and Gibson did likewise to the American League in the top of the ninth, the National League had just three outs left.

What miracle could the senior circuit pull off this time? Another last-ditch rally seemed unlikely as Manager Weaver brought in Catfish Hunter, who had been the victim of Perez' dramatic fifteenth-inning home run in 1967. Now, as the Catfish came in to pitch, the scoreboard showed that the National League had just three hits. Two of them were by Cubs' shortstop Don Kessinger, and the other by his replacement, Bud Harrelson of the Mets. And Harrelson had a hunch about that kind of situation.

"When the shortstops get the hits that belittles the big guys and they wake up," Harrelson said. "They figure they have to do something."

But it was the so-called little guys, or lesser known players, who started it all. The Giants' Dick Dietz was up first and Hunter immediately fell victim to his old whammy—the home run. Dietz hit one out to make it 4-2. Next came Harrelson and he promptly got his second hit, making it four for the shortstops. After Cito Gaston popped out, Joe Morgan of Houston singled Harrelson to second.

With Willie McCovey due up, Manager Weaver yanked Hunter and brought in Yankee left-hander Fritz Peterson. But the lefty vs. lefty strategy didn't work this time. McCovey ripped a base hit to center, scoring Harrelson with the third run and sending Morgan to third. Now the tying run was 90 feet away, and the game that was in the bag for the American League was no longer a lock. With Roberto Clemente stepping up as a pinch hitter, Weaver called for another Yankee, righty Mel Stottlemyre.

Clemente promptly lifted one in the air deep enough to score Morgan with the tying run. The sacrifice fly had completed yet another last-minute comeback that averted defeat for the Nationals. But they still hadn't won it. Stottlemyre worked out of the inning and for the sixth time the All-Star Game went into extras.

Extra innings have never been the American League's thing. In fact, the Nationals had won all five previous overtime games. It would have been interesting to take a poll of the American Leaguers right then and there. Confidence probably wasn't the byword right then. And when Claude Osteen of the Dodgers began setting the American League down, things must have looked bleak.

Stottlemyre pitched the tenth and the Angels' Clyde Wright took over in the eleventh. Both he and Osteen then pitched into the twelfth. Once again the Americans went down, and now the Nationals were up again. When Wright retired the first two hitters it looked as if the game would go to the thirteenth. But then the Cincinnati crowd began to buzz, and the buzz soon crescendoed into a roar. For coming to the plate was their hometown hero, Pete Rose. The man who was to become the most prolific hit producer in big-league history did his thing. He slammed a single.

When Dodger infielder Billy Grabarkewitz followed with another base hit, the crowd was on its feet. The next batter was Jim Hickman of the Cubs, and while no one could predict it, everyone watching was about to witness one of the most memorable moments in All-Star history. For Hickman picked out a Wright delivery and whacked a solid single to center field.

As center fielder Amos Otis charged the ball, Rose steamed around third and catcher Fosse took two steps in front of the plate to await the throw. Otis cut it loose and all three elements came together, as if anxious to keep their date with All-Star destiny. Whether Fosse could have put the tag on Rose will never really be known. For as the ball reached the plate, so did Rose, and he slammed into catcher Fosse at full speed, knocking the sturdy catcher backwards, leaving him slightly dazed.

It was this kind of drive and determination that allowed Pete Rose to score the winning run in the 1970 Game, knocking over catcher Ray Fosse to do it.

It had happened so quickly that it took a second for people to realize that Rose had scored the winning run and the National League had won. Again! They had taken a 5-4, twelve-inning verdict for their eighth straight All-Star win.

The collision at home plate had left Rose with a swollen knee and Fosse with a more serious shoulder injury. But Charley Hustle had no apologies.

"I started to slide headfirst, but I saw I couldn't make it because he was in front of the plate," Rose explained, afterward. "If I would have slid, I would have been out. The only thing I could do was run over him. That's the only way I know how to play. I play to win. I asked him if he was okay, but he had his head down. I hope he's okay."

The defeat was one of the most disheartening the American League had ever suffered. Manager Earl Weaver took part of the blame himself.

"Damn," he said. "So close. It's one thing to get killed, 14-3, but it come so close. When am I going to do something right for the American League?"

Weaver's third baseman, Brooks Robinson, put it in more analytical terms, and in doing so, admitted something that many people had already known.

"You know, in the early 1960s you had to admit to yourself that they [the National League] could put nine men on the field who had an edge over us," Robinson said. "I don't mean the whole league or anything. But they could field a better team of stars. But in the last two years, I really feel our team is as good as theirs, and that makes it harder to take when you lose, especially this way, in a close game."

For the American League, the rallying cry of "Wait till next year!" was wearing a little thin.

The 1971 Game

What would it take for the American League to win an All-Star Game? That seemed a logical question as the 1971 game approached. After all, no league had ever dominated to the tune of eight straight victories before, or had even come close. The year before the Nationals had done just about everything but hand the Americans the game on a platter. Then came the ninth inning and they took it back and turned it over to Pete Rose for his twelfth-inning heroics.

Now the teams would be meeting at Detroit's Tiger Stadium, a home run hitter's haven, and it seemed as if fireworks would be in the air. The question was how shellshocked were the American Leaguers after events of the past few years? Was it a matter of losing begets losing, or was the National League indeed the stronger league in terms of stars? A look at the All-Star rosters for 1971 once again seemed to favor the senior circuit. They had big blasters like the aging Mays, Clemente, Aaron, Lee May, Joe Torre, Ron Santo, Stargell, McCovey and Bench. These guys might find Tiger Stadium just what the doctor ordered.

The American League hoped it had a trump card this time, however. He was a hard-throwing, not yet 22-year-old left-hander with the unlikely name of Vida Blue. Blue had taken the American League by storm in 1971, and had won 17 games by the time the July 13 All-Star Game rolled around. He had an explosive fastball and a sharp-breaking curve, as well as the kind of command, or mound presence, that the great ones seem to have. With Blue the obvious choice to start the game, Manager Earl Weaver and the American League

The American League's big hope before the Game was twenty-one year old Vida Blue. But, alas, Blue's fastball was just a little too good, and after two home runs it looked like the American League had no hope.

squad hoped an overpowering performance from the young lefty would set the tone for a winning game.

The Nationals and Cincy manager Sparky Anderson seemed unconcerned. They started right-hander Dock Ellis, who was also having a fine year, and figured their hitters more than equal to the task. The first inning passed without incident. Blue set the Nationals down in 1-2-3 order and then

Ellis came out and got the Americans with little trouble. But in the second inning, those fireworks everyone had predicted began.

Blue started things off himself by plunking Willie Stargell with a pitch. Now Willie McCovey was up. The young left-hander reached back and fanned the Giants' first sacker. But then he had to face Cincy catcher Johnny Bench. This time Blue's fastball was a little too good and Bench crushed it, driving a two-run homer into the seats and giving the National League the early lead. But Blue's problems weren't over yet. In the top of the third, the great Henry Aaron, who had talked about his own problems in the All-Star Game several years before, caught hold of another high hard one and rode it into the seats for a home run. Now it was a 3-0 game and the American League hopes seemed to be fading into the sunset already. Some of the National League players were probably thinking blowout.

Ellis had already gone through two innings without problems and now he came out to face the Americans in the last of the third. In light of recent developments, oddsmakers probably wouldn't have given the American League much of a chance at a comeback. But whenever someone is standing at home plate with a bat in his hands there's a chance. And the junior circuit did have some fine players out there.

Luis Aparicio, now playing for the Red Sox, led off the third with a single. With Blue due next, manager Weaver went to his bench. Out of the dugout walked Oakland outfielder Reggie Jackson. Jackson had burst upon the baseball scene two years earlier when, in just his second full season, he had hit 39 home runs by the end of July. But a second half slump saw him hit only eight more the rest of the year. And he had more or less struggled ever since. In fact, he wasn't even

A Cincinnati All-Star infield—Concepcion, Bench, Morgan, and Rose.

picked to the squad in 1971 until an injury forced Weaver to add a player. Now that player was digging in from the left side of the plate to face Dock Ellis.

Ellis worked Jackson carefully, mixing a fastball with off-speed pitches. When he had two strikes on the young slugger, he tried to slip a fastball through. And that's when it happened. Jackson ripped at the ball and it left the bat as if jet-propelled. It rose majestically in the nighttime Detroit sky, headed to right center field. Mays and Aaron, playing center and right, took one step, then stopped and watched. The ball kept rising. In fact, it was still rising when it passed over the fence. Had it not struck a generator box atop a light tower in right center more than 500 feet from home plate, there's no telling how far the ball would have gone.

Jackson just stood at the plate and watched for a few seconds, then went into his home run trot. He had just hit one of the longest home runs ever, a shot that put both the fans and other players in awe of the power display they had witnessed.

"I can't remember seeing a ball hit that hard or that far," said Al Kaline, a regular performer at Tiger Stadium. "Too bad it hit that thing up there. I would have loved to have seen where it ended up."

And the Reds' Johnny Bench, who had already hit one off Blue, also marveled at Jackson's blast.

"I thought Reggie's drive was going to knock the whole tower down," Bench said. "I've never seen a ball take off that way."

A youthful Reggie Jackson slammed a mammoth homer to ignite the American League after Blue's luck ran out. The blast is considered one of the hardest hit homers ever.

Reggie himself tried to explain what happened. "I didn't want to strike out," he admitted, "and I wasn't trying for a home run. I just tried to meet the ball, but I do think it was the longest one I've ever hit. And the people amazed me. They were dumbstruck. They just sat there. They didn't even cheer."

Still shaken, Ellis walked Rod Carew, but settled down to get the next two hitters. Then he had to face former National Leaguer Frank Robinson. Robby picked on an outside fastball and sliced it into the right field seats for a two-run homer that gave the Americans a 4-3 lead. The homer enabled Robinson to become the first player to homer for both leagues in an All-Star Game competition, but that didn't matter as much as the fact that his blast had given the American League the lead. And he also spoke about how Jackson's blast had lifted the entire team.

"That was the thing that turned us around," Robinson said. "When he fell behind, 3-0, we said, 'Oh, no, here they go again.' But his homer picked us up."

With Blue gone, Jim Palmer and Mike Cuellar held the Nationals in check over the next three innings, while Juan Marichal hurled a pair of scoreless frames for the Nationals. Then came the bottom of the sixth with the Cubs' Ferguson Jenkins on the mound for the Nationals. Great as he was, Jenkins was another pitcher who had a tendency to throw gopher balls. And with one on, he threw one to Harmon Killebrew, who blasted it out and gave the junior circuit a 6-3 lead. Now the question was: Could the American League hold on, or would the Nationals find still another way to pull a rabbit out of their All-Star hat?

Cuellar finished his two-inning stint with another scoreless frame in the seventh, then gave way to Detroit left-hander

Mickey Lolich. He would have the unenviable task of trying to close the door on the National League, something American League pitchers had been unable to do in recent years.

There was a scare in the eighth when Roberto Clemente teed off a Lolich fastball and hit the game's record-tying sixth home run. That made it 6-4, and a two-run lead on the Nationals wasn't very safe. But Lolich pitched out of the eighth and with Houston's Don Wilson shutting down the American League, Lolich had to come out again in the ninth. Like the year before, the Americans were just three outs away from that elusive win.

This time they weren't about to let it get away. Lolich disposed of the Nationals in 1-2-3 fashion and the Americans had themselves a victory, their first in nine years. Junior circuit pitchers had shut the National League down on just five

Frank Robinson, the only player to win the Most Valuable Player prize in both leagues, did his thing for the Americans in 1971 with a home run.

Roberto Clemente of the Pirates had one of six home runs hit in the 1971 Game.

hits, despite the fact that the senior circuit had roughed up their best pitcher, Vida Blue. But the game's hero and Blue's teammate, Reggie Jackson, had an explanation for that.

"He [Blue] was facing the cream of the crop," Jackson

said. "These fellows are the best there are. He made two mistakes, one to Bench and the other to Aaron. When you make mistakes with those guys, you pay your dues."

Sparky Anderson, who became the National League's first losing All-Star manager in nearly a decade, once again told of his players' desire to participate in and win the mid-summer classic. First he apologized for not getting Pirates' catcher Manny Sanguillen in the game.

"After Johnny Bench, I think Sanguillen is the best catcher in baseball," Sparky said, "and he certainly deserved to play. I kept looking for a spot, but just couldn't find one."

"I know what it means to all these men, how they feel about being in the game," the manager said. "Look at Willie McCovey, how badly he wanted to play. He has a knee that's so bad, he has no business being here."

So the streak was broken. Some of the National Leaguers had never lost an All-Star Game before, just as some of the American Leaguers had never won one. If nothing else, the American League finally proved it could win again. It would be a lesson that the players from the junior circuit would have a hard time remembering. For it would be more than a decade before the junior circuit tasted victory once more. The Nationals were about to work their magic as they never worked it before.

The 1972 Game

Like most streaks in baseball, this one started slowly and unassumingly, with no real fanfare or definitive statement. But coming off their long sought after victory in 1971, the American League surely came into the 1972 game on a high note. After all, now it was up to the Nationals to reverse their fortunes. And perhaps the Americans could start a little run of their own.

With the teams gathering at Atlanta Stadium, Earl Weaver would be running the American League for the third straight year, while Pittsburgh's Danny Murtaugh led the Nationals. Before this one even started, there was some controversy, and it again pointed up the tremendous pride some players took in participating in the game. To be in the starting line-up was a kind of recognition of their achievements during the regular season.

Thus when Earl Weaver named Baltimore's Jim Palmer as the American League starter, Detroit's Mickey Lolich suddenly proclaimed that he would not pitch in the game. Lolich had been one of the American League's best pitchers in 1971 with a 25-14 record and 308 strikeouts. He was also the pitcher who saved the American League's first win in nine years and was on his way to another 20-win year. He felt he deserved the honor of being the All-Star starter and finally talked to reporters about it.

"I was fuming and I was hurt when I said I wouldn't pitch," he explained. "I said I thought the guy with the most wins should start. He [manager Weaver] told me I was going to be the middle man and it sounded like I was being sloughed off, if it's possible to be sloughed off in an All-Star Game.

National League All-Stars Joe Morgan, Don Kessinger, and Johnny Bench huddle under an umbrella before the start of a regular season game in 1972.

"After I hung up I was sitting in my room with my wife, and after a few minutes I said to her, 'That's stupid. It's an honor to be here.' But I still think I should have started."

Palmer, who was tabbed to take the hill, refused to become embroiled in the controversy. A normally low-key guy anyway, Palmer responded to questions about the starting pitcher by saying simply, "I'd rather be in Ocean City"—a popular Maryland resort.

But when the game began, Palmer was the one to take the mound and Lolich was available in the bullpen. On the

Always an intense competitor, Bob Gibson blanked the Americans for the first two innings of the 1972 Game.

The always-dangerous Rod Carew.

mound for the Nationals was the combative Bob Gibson. And once again, a quick scan of the rosters gave the impression that the Nationals had the more powerful team.

Yet for the first two innings, neither team did much. Palmer, as he had in the past, was pitching brilliantly. But so was Gibson. Murtaugh yanked Gibby after two and brought in his own star right-hander, Steve Blass, who had been the World Series hero the year before. But the Americans Leaguers weren't interested in past performance.

Blass started by walking catcher Bill Freehan, who was then sacrificed to second by Palmer. That brought up the dangerous Rod Carew, who promptly slapped a single to drive home Freehan with the first run of the game. Maybe the Americans did have something going for them after all.

After the pitching three strong innings, Palmer gave way to the reluctant Lolich, who followed with an equally strong pair of frames, and at the end of five it was still a 1-0 game. Don Sutton of the Dodgers had hurled the last two for the Nationals and had also looked very strong.

Then in the sixth, the Americans had to face lefty Steve Carlton, who was in the midst of one of the greatest mound seasons in recent memory. Carlton was on his way to compiling a 27-10 record with a 1.97 ERA, 30 complete games, and 310 strikeouts. And he was doing it for a last-place Phillies team that would finish with a 59-97 record. Without Carlton pitching, the team was 32-87. That's how good he was.

Big Steve had no trouble with the American League in the sixth, and then the Nationals came up to face Gaylord Perry, a transplanted National Leaguer who was now pitching in Cleveland. Perry's first inning of work suddenly took a dramatic turn when the veteran right-hander had to face Henry

Old Henry hit "the most dramatic home run of his carrer," in the 1972 All-Star Game.

Tug McGraw always knew how to celebrate a win or a save. He was with the Phils here, but when he won the 1972 All-Star Game, he was still with the New York Mets.

Aaron with Cesar Cedeno on first. On the one hand, Aaron had always been a disappointing All-Star performer, with a .183 batting average and just one lone home run in twenty previous games. But on the other hand, Bad Henry was playing before his hometown fans, and they roared when the familiar number 44 ambled up to the plate.

A further irony. Just the year before, Aaron had hit the 600th home run of his career off the same Gaylord Perry, who was then still with the Giants. So it was strength against strength, and this time Aaron won, taking a Perry pitch deep into the left field stands for a two-run homer that gave the Nationals a one-run lead.

Afterward, Aaron would call the shot "the most dramatic home run of my career," and when asked what kind of pitch he hit, he said, "The ball I hit was a spitter, but not one of his best spitters."

Perry, always in a swirl of controversy over whether he loaded the ball or not, simply said, "Fastball, inside."

Whatever it was, it gave the Nationals the lead and now the American League had to play from behind, something they had not excelled at in recent years. So they waited until the eighth inning. Then, facing the Expos' Bill Stoneman, they went to work, getting a pair of runs courtesy of a most unlikely source.

Boston's Carlton Fisk began it with a single. After the next batter had been retired, Rod Carew was due up. But Carew had suffered a rib-cage injury earlier in the game and now Cookie Rojas of the Royals was coming in to pinch hit. Rojas was a good infielder for both the Phillies and Kansas City Royals during his career. But he was hardly considered an All-Star in the classic sense. His lifetime batting average was just .263 and the most home runs he ever hit in a single season was nine.

Joe Morgan of Cincinnati is all smiles as he receives congratulations from National League teammates following his game-winning single in the tenth inning.

So what happened? Only the most unlikely thing of all. Cookie Rojas took Bill Stoneman downtown, clubbing a clutch two-run homer that gave the Americans a 3-2 lead. Now, the Nationals had just six outs to try to get even. And they would be facing a tough hombre in left-handed knuckleballer Wilbur Wood of the White Sox. Wood was in the midst of a 24-win season with the Pale Hose and when his knuckler was working, he was one of the best. In the eighth, Wood got the Nationals without much trouble. If he could do it once more, the Americans would have back-to-back wins for the first time since 1957 and 1958.

But it seemed that whenever the National Leaguers had their backs against the wall, they were at their best. The Americans had to be wondering why it was always so difficult getting those last three outs. For it happened again in 1972.

Wood went to work, but Billy Williams lashed a singled to start things off. Manny Sanguillen was next, and the free-swinging catcher sliced a base hit to right, sending the tying run in the form of Williams around to third. The Reds' Lee May then bounced into a forceout, but Williams flashed across home plate with the run that evened the score at three. Wood then pitched out of the inning, but the damage had been done. The Nationals had tied it and sent the All-Star Game into extra innings for the seventh time. And there wasn't a player on either team who wasn't well aware of the results of the previous six.

New York Mets left-hander Tug McGraw had pitched a scoreless ninth for the Nationals and he was back on the mound as the tenth inning got underway. The exuberant McGraw played the game with the joy and verve of a kid. His energy and enthusiasm were boundless. Before the game he had gone up to manager Murtaugh and said, "I appreciate being here."

Murtaugh answered without hesitation. "You earned it."

But McGraw really did appreciate his first taste of All-Star action. As usual, he didn't try to hide his feelings. "I started getting nervous when they introduced Mays and Aaron before the game," he said. "That got to me and I realized where I was."

Where he was now was the mound at Atlanta, and what he was doing was using his fastball and screwball to set the Americans down once again. Now his teammates came up in the bottom of the inning to face Orioles left-hander Dave McNally, who was coming in for his first inning of work.

When McNally walked leadoff batter Nate Colbert, he was already in trouble. Playing for a single run, Murtaugh had the Giants' Chris Speier sacrifice Colbert to second. That brought up Joe Morgan, in his first season with Cincinnati after being traded to the Reds from Houston. "Little Joe," who would become one of the best all-around players of his generation, quickly sent a base hit to right center. Colbert scored easily and the Nationals were cheering again. They had won their seventh extra-inning All-Star Game, 4-3, and had erased the loss suffered the year before.

For the Americans, it was yet another heartbreaking All-Star defeat, a scenario that was becoming all too habit-forming. The Nationals were now ahead in the series, 24-18, and while they didn't know it at the time, the best was yet to come. It really was.

The 1979 Game

Frustration had to be the byword for the American League by the time the 1979 All-Star Game rolled around. Their fortunes hadn't been good. When they had broken the Nationals' eight-game win streak in 1971, many American League players an fans probably felt it would never happen again. The law of averages, for one thing, wouldn't allow it. Yet coming into the 1979 midsummer classic, the American League had once again lost seven straight All-Star Games.

And suddenly they weren't so close anymore. The scores from 1973 to 1978 were 7-1, 7-2, 6-3, 7-1, 7-5, 7-3. Seems the Nationals liked that lucky number 7. But not only was it seven in a row. Counting that earlier win streak, the senior circuit had now won fifteen of the sixteen games, an almost incredible run. This time, the two star-studded teams would be meeting in the Seattle Kingdome. The game would be perhaps the most exciting in eight years, and would prove all over again that there really seemed to be some kind of magic in that old National League hat.

Interestingly enough, the starting pitchers in 1979 would go on to become the two greatest strikeout pitchers in major league history. For the American League, fastballer Nolan Ryan, then with the California Angels, got the call. Ryan was one of the hardest-throwing pitchers to ever pull on a uniform, and he was well on his way to breaking nearly every existing strikeout mark in major league annals.

Opposing the California right-hander was veteran southpaw Steve Carlton, whose wicked, sharp-breaking slider was the bane of many a National League hitter over the years.

Nolan Ryan, one of the hardest-throwing pitchers to ever pull on a uniform.

Surely, Carlton would get the Nationals off to a fast start and on the way to a record-tying eighth straight win.

To the surprise of everyone, neither Ryan nor Carlton had his good stuff and it was the hitters on both teams who got off to the quick start. It began in the top of the first. Ryan came out and blew smoke past the Dodgers' Davey Lopes and Pittsburgh's Dave Parker. But just when it looked like a 1-2-3 frame, the hard-throwing righty walked L.A.'s Steve Garvey. Philadelphia third baseman Mike Schmidt was next and he slammed a long triple, scoring Garvey. When Cincy's George Foster followed with a double, the Nationals had a 2-0 lead and seemed off to the races once more.

But Steve Carlton fared no better than Ryan when it was his turn on the hill. A one-out walk to K.C.'s George Brett started the American League comeback. Don Baylor of the Angels picked up Brett by whacking a double, and when Boston's Fred Lynn slammed one over the right center field fence, the American League had come right back for a 3-2 lead.

Ryan then went out to try again. But three singles and a sacrifice fly by Parker tied the game at three. So in the space of an inning and a half, two of the game's great pitchers were gone, having giving up a combined six runs. Houston's Joaquin Andujar held the Americans in the second, and in the third the Nationals got another off Boston's Bob Stanley when Schmidt doubled and came home on two ground balls.

The see-saw affair continued. With Andujar still on the mound in the bottom of the third, it was the Americans' turn. A Baylor single, followed by a wild pitch, a groundout, a hit batter, then a single by Carl Yastrzemski got the tying run home. Moments later, a Schmidt throwing error allowed a second run to score and after just three innings of a wild and wooly game, the Americans led, 5-4.

Things had to settle down, and they did in the fourth and fifth. Steve Rogers of Montreal did the pitching in those frames for the National, while Stanley and Mark Clear of the

Mike Schmidt of the Phils was one of the National League superstars who helped the senior circuit to its eleven straight All-Star victories. In 1979, Schmidt had two hits,

Angels hurled the goose eggs for the American League. But the quiet didn't last for long. In the sixth, the Nationals tied it against Clear when Dave Winfield of the Padres slammed a double and Montreal's Gary Carter singled him home. That made it a 5-5 game.

Veteran Gaylord Perry, now back in the National League with the Padres, came in to pitch the bottom of the sixth. But he didn't last long. Three straight singles, the last by Seattle's Bruce Bochte, gave the American League the lead once again at 6-5, and sent Perry to an early shower. Joe Sambito of Houston and Cincy's Mike LaCoss both came in to stem the American League tide, with no more runs crossing the plate.

But how many times had this been the scenario in recent years? The American League had a lead going into the late innings and the Nationals were trying to catch them. They couldn't do it in the seventh, but in the bottom of the inning the Americans saw a chance for some insurance—almost.

Jim Rice led off against LaCoss and hit a fly ball down the right field line. It should have been a fairly routine play for Dave Parker, but he lost the ball in the lights. Running hard all the way, Rice rounded second and headed for third. Parker picked the ball up and uncorked a laser-like throw to third baseman Roy Cey that just nipped the sliding Rice by a whisker. With none out, the odds are that Parker's great throw saved a run. The big guy described how it happened.

"I lost the ball in the ceiling, but it took a hop up to me," Parker said. "I figured he must be somewhere near third base and I just fired. You know, if you're not hitting, you've got to do something else."

Parker's throw saved an almost certain run, and it also might have helped ignite the Nationals. In the eighth, Dodger Manager Tom LaSorda sent up a pinch hitter, the Mets' Lee

Mazzilli, to bat for Atlanta's Gary Matthews. With Texas right-hander Jim Kern on the mound, LaSorda wanted the left handed bat of the switch-hitting Mazzilli. So what happened? Maz stroked one to the opposite field, a high drive down the left field line that just cleared the fence inside the foul pole for a game-tying home run. An upset Jim Kern would later call it a "317-foot-fly down a 316-foot-line." But the damage was done.

Now the game was tied and moving into the bottom of the eighth. The Americans were well aware of the Nationals' late-inning lightning, as well as their own futile, oh-fer, record in extra inning affairs. They knew they needed to do something in the last of the eighth.

Facing Cubs' relief ace Bruce Sutter, the Angels' Brian Downing led things off with a base hit. Now the American League bench came alive. It was almost a now-or-never situation for them, even though the score was still tied. Playing for the run, Manager Bob Lemon of the Yankees ordered a sacrifice, which moved Downing to second. Now all the wheels were turning. LaSorda had Sutter walk slugger Reggie Jackson intentionally. Sutter then got the second out, but still had to face the dangerous Graig Nettles of the Yanks.

Nettles picked out one of the Sutter's split-fingered fastballs and slammed a solid single to right. As Downing chugged around third it looked as if he would score the go-ahead tally. But there was right fielder Parker again, fielding the ball and uncorking one of the most amazing throws in All-Star history. The ball seemed self-propelled as it came in to catcher Gary Carter on a low line. Carter blocked the plate beautifully, forcing Downing to the outside, and then tagged him to complete the play. Once again the Americans had been stopped by a bit of National League magic. "I got a good grip on the ball and wanted to throw it low and on a bounce," Parker said. "But it carried all the way in and Gary blocked the plate and made a sensational tag."

Manager LaSorda also couldn't say enough about the big right fielder."It [the throw] looked like it was shot out of the cannon," the manager said. "That's why I would have kept Parker in this game if it had gone twenty innings."

But it was only the ninth, with the Nationals coming up to face Jim Kern, and when Kern walked the Reds' Joe Morgan and then balked him to second, the Americans must have sensed the end being near. But they weren't about to quit. Lemon ordered Parker walked intentionally. Kern then bore down and retired the next two hitters. But when he walked Ron Cey to load the bases, Lemon came out and gave Kern the hook. He signalled for Yankee left hander Ron Guidry, precipitating another bit of controversy.

Guidry, a whippet-thin left-hander, had been the talk of baseball the year before, In just his second full season, the Yankee southpaw had compiled an amazing 25-3 record with a 1.74 ERA and nine shutouts. He was clearly the best pitcher

Big Dave Parker showed you don't have to hit to win ball games. His two brilliant throws from right field insured the Nationals of another victory in 1979.

in baseball that season. In 1979 he was still a force and seemed like a logical choice in that situation—except Guidry had thrown a tough complete game just two days before in California. He didn't feel he was ready.

"I told Lem before the game that I could give him one or two batters," Guidry said. "But then I was up [throwing in the bullpen] three times, and I can't do that after pitching nine innings Sunday. I didn't have anything when I came in, and said so to Graig Nettles when I walked past him to the mound."

From his perspective, Manager Lemon felt he had done the right thing.

"I saw him pitch in that situation earlier in the year and he did a good job. He's a strikeout pitcher and when he came in, we needed a strikeout."

And that brought still an added piece of drama. The hitter Lemon wanted Guidry to strike out was Lee Mazzilli, who had hit the game-tying homer an inning earlier. And

"Little Joe" Morgan—one of the best all-around players of his generation.

Mazzilli saw the confrontation as something more than pitcher versus hitter.

"I knew if they walked Ron Cey ahead of me Guidry would come in," he said. "The only time I faced him was in spring training. But as far as I was concerned, it was the battle of New York, me against Guidry."

Without his good stuff, which included a wicked slider that caused hitters to fan in the breeze, Guidry struggled. Mazzilli ran the count to 2-0, then 3-1. Guidry delivered again. Ball four! Mazzilli had walked, and in doing so forced the go-ahead run across the plate.

Though Guidry then retired the next hitter, the damage had been done. Sutter made quick work of the Americans in the bottom of the inning, closing the door and allowing the Nationals to take a 7-6, come-from-behind victory, as well as a record-tying eighth straight All-Star triumph. Oh, when, oh, when, would the American League ever win again?

Pete Rose, that peripatetic National League wonder, set a rather unique All-Star record after playing the final four innings at first base. It was the fifth position Rose had played in All-Star competition. The others were second, third, right and left field. Old Charley Hustle would have probably even caught if someone had only asked.

The 1983 Game

Fast forward to 1983 and there were no smiling faces in the American League, at least not where the All-Star Game was concerned. For the Nationals were still at it. They had run their winning streak to an incredible eleven straight games with victories from 1980-82, including another come-from-behind triumph in 1981. What had happened in the midsummer classic was absolutely amazing.

The National League had won nineteen of the last twenty games. For nearly two decades they had been almost unbeatable and had run their overall advantage to 33-18 with that one tie. It was even more incredible when you stopped to think about it. A single game in the middle of the baseball season with the top starters from each league. Oddsmakers would probably say the game should be close to a 50-50 proposition. Sure, there might be some player advantages, but that could easily be negated by a break here, a break there, or just one or two players who happened to be hot in a single game. But for one team to completely dominate in such a way has to be considered one of the strangest occurrences in all of sport.

Perhaps, just perhaps, 1983 would be different. After all, it marked the 50th anniversary of the star-studded event, and to commemorate that occasion the game was played in ancient Comiskey Park, the place where it all began back in 1933. Maybe the players from the junior circuit could evoke some of the ghosts from the American League past, when players like the Babe, old Double XX, the Iron Horse, Joe D. and the Splendid Splinter helped the Americans to dominate the early years of the contest.

So the motivation was there and the Americans must have felt it, too. For even before the game started, Al Oliver of the Expos, a lifelong National Leaguer, observed, "I sensed something different about them," Oliver said. "You could see it on the field. They weren't smiling. They had their game faces on."

The opposing managers were Whitey Herzog of the Cardinals and Harvey Kuenn of the Milwaukee Brewers. They named Mario Soto of the Reds and Dave Stieb of the Toronto Blue Jays as the starting pitchers as the ballgame got underway. Within minutes the American League looked to be headed in the wrong direction again, courting defeat for the twelfth straight time.

Lead off man Steve Sax of the Dodgers hit a roller down the first base line that Stieb promptly threw away for an error. Then the speedy Sax swiped second. When Tim Raines of the Expos hit a second squibber down first, Stieb did it again, throwing it away for error number two, allowing Sax to come around to score with Raines rambling into third. Thoughts of a big inning must have gone through National League minds, but to his credit, Stieb didn't rattle after his two errors. He fanned Andre Dawson, Dale Murphy and Mike Schmidt, with an Al Oliver walk in between, to get out of the inning with no further damage.

Then in the bottom of the first the American League got a gift of its own. Rod Carew singled and Fred Lynn walked. But when Jim Rice hit a ball to Schmidt that had double play written all over it, the National League seemed safe—that is, until Schmidt bobbled the ball, and seconds later George Brett cracked a sacrifice fly to get the tying run across. In the second, the American League got another on a Dave Winfield (he was now with the Yanks) double, a throwing error by Sax,

Rod Carew waved his magic bat in the 1983 Game.

and a sacrifice fly by Milwaukee's Robin Yount. But that was just a preview of things to come. In the third, the Americans would put together the single biggest inning in All-Star history.

Left-hander Atlee Hammaker of the Giants had stepped to the mound to start the frame for the Nationals. Hammaker had come into the game a hot pitcher, with a league-leading 1.70 ERA. He was not greeted very kindly, however, when

Jim Rice started things off by poling a long home run. George Brett was next, and he promptly tripled to deep center. That should have been a tipoff on Hammaker's stuff right then and there.

But when Ted Simmons of the Brewers popped out, a sense of security probably returned to the National League dugout. But it was a false sense of security. For Dave Winfield then singled home Brett and Manny Trillo's base hit sent Winfield to second. Hammaker managed to get the second out, but he was still a long way from being out of the woods.

George Brett of the Royals.

Rod Carew waved his magic bat to the tune of an RBI single, with Trillo going to third and Carew to second on the throw home. Manager Herzog then ordered the right-handed hitting Robin Yount walked so that Hammaker could pitch to fellow lefty Fred Lynn with the bases loaded.

Lynn worked the count to 2-2, then whacked a Hammaker offering deep into the right field seats for the first ever grand-slam home run in All-Star history. That gave the Americans a record-setting seven-run inning and ran the score to 9-1, as Hammaker left the mound in favor of Bill Dawley. Lynn's blast had not only given the American League a big lead, but had really done something more for the beleaguered American Leaguers.

"The National League streak was something I couldn't understand," said American League President Lee McPhail. "It was very frustrating. But when I saw Fred Lynn's grand slam, I felt very, very good."

Fred Lynn's grand-slam homer was the first in All-Star Game history.

"We all knew about the exploding scoreboard and fireworks at Comiskey," said Dave Winfield. "We wanted to see some of them, and we did."

As for the victim of the explosion, Atlee Hammaker, he made no excuses whatsoever. "To put it bluntly," he said, "it's probably the worst exhibition of pitching you'll ever see."

Of course, the game wasn't over yet. And when the Nationals got single runs in the fourth and fifth off Rick Honeycutt of Texas, a few people began getting nervous. That made it 9-3, and with the National League's reputation for miracles, well, you can't blame the nay-sayers.

But this one was the American League's year. In the bottom of the seventh they got another pair, with the big blows being a triple by Detroit's Lou Whitaker and a double by Willie Wilson of Kansas City. And when they got two more in the eighth off Lee Smith of Chicago, that brought the score up to 13-3, an All-Star record for total runs, and it put the game in the bag.

When it ended, the American Leaguers had fifteen hits to go with their thirteen runs and a long-awaited feeling of vindication.

"It didn't matter if it was the 50th anniversary or the 100th," said Fred Lynn, who now had four All-Star Game homers, "I'm just happy we finally won one."

Harvey Kuenn, who had done what only other one American League manager had been able to do in the last twenty games, said he hadn't given his team any special kind of strategy.

"I told them to go out and hit and have some fun," he said. "My game is hitting, not holding meetings. So we hit, we set some scoring records, we proved there is no big difference between the leagues. And we put an end to a terrible strain.

Now *we* won the last game and we're back to square one."

"When we come back next year we won't have to listen to questions about why the National League is dominant," added Dave Winfield.

For the Phils' Mike Schmidt, the game was something of a transition for the National League, though it was pretty tough to explain away a ten run loss.

"Basically we had a pretty inexperienced team this year," Schmidt said, "one with a lot of young players. Not to make excuses, but a lot guys who were involved in the eleven straight wins weren't here tonight. We have pretty much to start over."

In a sense, Schmidt was right. Players like Mays, Aaron, Clemente, Williams, Stargell, Brock, Bench and Rose were not there. But, heck, for eleven years prior to the 1983 game, it didn't seem to matter who played. Just represent the National League and you'd win.

But for the American League, the 50th anniversary game had been a rousing success. The finality of the outcome and the way it happened served as at least a one-year vindication. With some forty-one Hall of Famers and eighty-eight former All-Stars in attendance, the Americans had shown they were fully capable of generating an explosion. The amazing thing is that it hadn't happened sooner. And the next logical question was, when would it happen again?

In a sense, the big blowout of 1983 set up a good deal of drama for the 1984 game. Would the American League be able to start a winning streak of its own? Was the makeup of the two leagues finally changing, with the momentum swinging back to the junior circuit? These were questions that would not be answered in a single year, but over a number of seasons.

Big Dave Winfield.

    After all, an eleven game winning streak was not something that was built in a day.

The 1984 and 1986 Games

Mike Schmidt was right about one thing. The face of the All-Stars was changing. The 1984 game was marked by the appearance of twenty-three first-time All-Stars on both ballclubs, and that means a lot of young players who might not have been aware of the pressures and traditions of the previous games. It's been said that fewer and fewer of today's young players have an awareness of the game's past and the players who came before them. Though certainly the fortunes of the two leagues in recent All-Star Games had been widely documented.

The scene of the 1984 game was an interesting one. It began with a return to those thrilling days of 1961, when Stu Miller was blown off the mound at Candlestick Park. That's right, the game was back in San Francisco, though the ballpark had been somewhat closed in with the addition of more seating in the outfield, so hopefully the winds would also behave better.

Paul Owens of the Phillies and Joe Altobelli of the Orioles were the opposing managers and they had the task of handling the young players, many of whom were somewhat awed by their first appearance in the midsummer classic.

"You never know if you'll have another chance next year," said Don Mattingly of the Yanks, in his first full season and on his way to a batting title. "If something ever happened in my life, running into a fence, messing up my knee, it's great to make it one time. It's exciting and a good feeling."

Another first-time player, Alvin Davis of Seattle, was

Don Mattingly, on his way to a batting title in his first full season, thought it was exciting to be on the All-Star team.

even more awestruck just being there. "When the season started I thought I'd be in Salt Lake City for the All-Star break, just watching it on TV," he said. "I just found out Friday I'd be here and it really took a while to sink in."

"It's a scary feeling, just walking in to the dressing room," Mattingly added. "This isn't like Triple A ball. I've never seen crowds like this."

But the veteran ballplayers were thinking about something else. Because baseball had become such big business in recent years, with escalating salaries the result of huge television contracts, the game was so often at the mercy of the corporate types who ran the networks. To get the game on prime time in the eastern markets, it had to begin after five p.m. on the West Coast. Not a time conducive to hitting.

"I thought it would be a low-scoring game," said veteran Steve Garvey. "When you look at the quality of the pitching staffs and the time of day, you know there won't be a lot of runs. One of the hardest times to hit is sunset. You lose the ball in the shadows."

And longtime National League catcher Gary Carter voiced similar sentiments. "You add a little twilight to those arms out there and you're going to get a lot of strikeouts."

Neither of the starters, Dave Stieb for the Americans and the Expos' Charlie Lea for the Nationals, was considering a big strikeout pitcher. They each got a pair in two innings of work, but they were also touched up for a total of six hits, something that wasn't expected in the late afternoon light.

The Nationals scored in the first when Garvey rapped a two-out single and took second on a Reggie Jackson error. Dale Murphy of the Braves then singled to right and when Garvey slammed into catcher Lance Parrish, the ball squirted away for another error and the National League had a run. But in the second, the Royals' George Brett got it back with one swing, stroking a home run off Lea to tie the game at 1-1.

Then in the bottom of the inning Gary Carter slammed his third All-Star homer to give his club the lead against at 2-1. And that's when the pitching finally took command. Dodger lefty Fernando Valenzuela came on in the third for the Nationals, as did Jack Morris of Detroit for the American League.

Valenzuela had burst on the scene in the strike-shortened season of 1981, and had captured the fancy of the baseball world with a kind of charisma all his own. The portly left-hander didn't look like an athlete, but he had a unique style of pitching that saw him roll his eyes toward the heavens before delivering the baseball. He also had a screwball that often left right-handed hitters swinging at air.

Fernando Valenzuela used his famous screwball and pitched two strong innings in 1984, and struck out five straight American Leaguers in 1986.

The Mexican native pitched two strong innings, striking out three, as the Nationals held onto their lead. Morris, a twenty game winner in 1983, also pitched shutout ball, fanning two. But it was the way Valenzuela got his three K's that captured the fancy of the fans. In his first inning of work he didn't strike out a hitter, but in the fourth, he put the scroogie to work and got Dave Winfield, Reggie Jackson, and George Brett in succession. It made some think back to 1934, when the Giants' Carl Hubbell had used a screwball to set an All-Star record by fanning Ruth, Gehrig, Foxx, Simmons and Cronin in order.

But Fernando would not get a chance to tie or break that mark, for in the fifth inning, Dwight Gooden was standing out on the mound. If Valenzuela was the sensation of 1981, Gooden was the main man in 1984. Just nineteen years old, Gooden was a rookie with the New York Mets, a rookie possessing a blazing fastball and a curve that looked like it was falling off a table. He also had poise, the kind that would add up to a 17-9 rookie record, with a league-leading 276 strikeouts.

Gooden not only became the youngest player ever to appear in an All-Star Game, he took right up where Valenzuela left off, striking out Lance Parrish, Chet Lemon, and Alvin Davis, and making it a record six-straight strikeouts for the National League. Manager Owens was certainly impressed with the Mets' rookie.

"He's a terrific young pitcher," Owens said. "He's got the high hard heater and there's no one I can compare him with. There's certainly no nineteen year-old like him."

The two young pitchers set the tone for the rest of the game. The Nationals got a final tally in the eighth when Dale Murphy homered off Willie Hernandez of Detroit. Mario

Doctor K, Dwight Gooden, the youngest player, at nineteen, to play in the All-Star Game.

Soto of Cincinnati and Rich "Goose" Gossage of San Diego finished the job by preserving the Nationals' 3-1 victory. And Joe Altobelli had been right. There were a lot of strikeouts, twenty-one to be exact, a record for a nine-inning game, with eleven of them recorded by National League pitchers.

So after just a one-year hiatus, the senior circuit was back on track.

Roger Clemens retired nine-straight National Leaguers in the 1986 Game. The Rocket Man was great.

They did it again the next year, winning rather easily, 6-1, and leading baseball people to wonder if another streak was in the offing. So many people looked to the 1986 game at the Houston Astrodome as a barometer of things to come.

Once again there were a number of young players in attendance, but as in 1984, the emphasis was on pitching. The Nationals started Dwight Gooden, who was coming off an incredible 1985 season in which he was 24-4. The Americans went with Roger Clemens of Boston, who was in the midst of a superb season. The Rocket Man, as he was called, was not yet twenty-four years old, and en route to duplicating Gooden's 24-4 log of a year earlier. Coming into the All-Star Game, Clemens had an amazing 15-2 mark, including a game in which he fanned a record 20 batters. So the pitching matchup was looked upon with great anticipation.

As it turned out, the Rocket Man was great. Pitching before his home state fans in Texas, Clemens breezed through the National League line-up, retiring nine straight with apparent ease. He only fanned a pair, but the incredible part was that of the twenty-five pitches he threw, twenty-one of them were strikes. His command couldn't have been better.

Gooden, on the other hand, ran into some trouble in the second inning. The Doctor, as he was now called, allowed a double to the Yanks' Dave Winfield, and then was touched for a two-run homer off the bat of Detroit's Lou Whitaker. He then settled down to finish his three-inning stint.

But the pitchers continued to dominate. Milwaukee's Teddy Higuera, who some say pitches like Valenzuela, followed Clemens with three innings of one-hit ball. Only he was overshadowed by the man he supposedly emulated. Fernando came on for Gooden in the fourth and started throwing the screwball.

In that inning, he fanned Mattingly, Cal Ripken of Baltimore, and Toronto's Jesse Barfield. And this time he had a chance to come out for the following frame. Not wasting any time, Valenzuela promptly tied Hubbell's All-Star record by striking out Whitaker and Higuera for five in a row. Kirby

Puckett of the Twins ended the string with a groundout.

"After I was removed for a pinch hitter," Fernando said, "I looked at the scoreboard and saw that I had tied the record. But I don't know about Carl Hubbell. I was born in 1960. But I was very lucky to strike out five in a row. I do not try to strike out everyone. I'm very happy for the record because everyone knows the name of Carl Hubbell and to tie his record is an honor."

"He's got a good screwball, a fastball, and a sharp breaking curve," said Mattingly of Valenzuela. "His screwball breaks like a right-hander's breaking ball. It's a good pitch."

Through six, the National League had just a single hit, and that wasn't your ordinary, everyday All-Star occurrence. Then in the top of the seventh, the American League got what appeared to be an insurance run when Kansas City secondsacker Frank White drove a Mike Scott pitch into the left field seats. That made it 3-0. Was it the calm before the storm, or would the American League pitchers continue to stymie the hitters from the senior circuit?

The problems started in the bottom of the eighth as Texas knuckleballer Charlie Hough began his second inning of work. Hough had done a 1-2-3 number on the Nationals in the seventh, but in the eighth it started coming apart. Chris Brown of the Giants started things off with a double, only the National League's second hit. Hough then worked his knuckleball magic on Chili Davis, also from the Giants, striking him out. But catcher Rich Gedman of the Red Sox couldn't hold on to the flutterball. Though he grabbed it to throw Davis out at first, Brown went over to third.

Hough then fanned Hubie Brooks, but Gedman again failed to hold onto the ball. Brown scored, Brooks ran to first, and then took second on a balk. After Hough struck out Tim Raines of Montreal, Gedman holding the ball this time, the Dodgers' Steve Sax rapped a base hit to score Brooks with the second run. Manager Dick Howser then pulled Hough and brought in the Yanks' Dave Righetti, who retired the side. But it was now a 3-2 game.

In the ninth, the Nationals tried it again. They put runners at the corners with one out as Baltimore's Don Aase replaced Righetti. With the tying run and the potential for one of those extra inning games just 90 feet away, Aase got Chris Brown to hit a check-swing grounder to Frank White at second, who stepped on the bag and fired to first for a game-ending doubleplay.

So the American League had won it, their second victory in the past four years. Playing the Nationals to a standoff was a lot better than losing eleven in a row. Frank White, whose homer proved to be the winning run, talked about being an unlikely hero. "You come into this game and see all the great players, so you have an idea in your mind about who the stars might be. But in this game, you never know."

As for MVP Roger Clemens, his first All-Star Game was almost too good to be true. "It was a thrill to win the MVP," he said, "especially at home in front of so much family and so many friends. This whole year has been like a fantasy camp for me."

The 1984 and 1986 games featured a number of brilliant young pitchers at their awesome best. Was there a new pattern developing, one in which hard-throwing youngsters pitching against hitters for the first time had a big advantage? It was a distinct possibility.

The 1987 Game

In 1987, baseballs were flying out of major league ballparks at a record rate. The proliferation of the long ball sparked a lively debate about the possibility of a livelier baseball. Was it juiced up? Naturally, with all this long ball mania at work, it was no surprise when the National and American League All-Star squads gathered at the Oakland-Alameda County Coliseum on July 14, that many people were predicting little more than a home-run hitting contest.

The host team Oakland, in fact, had two of the hottest young home run hitters in the game. One was Jose Canseco, a huge, Cuban-born outfielder who had blasted 33 en route to a Rookie of the Year season in 1986. And in 1987, Canseco had a teammate who was even hotter. His name was Mark McGwire, and by All-Star time, the 6'5" first baseman had 33 round trippers, putting him just five homers away from the rookie record of 38. He would wind up with 49 for the year.

Managers John McNamara of the Red Sox and Davey Johnson of the Mets, had many of those young home run hitters ready to go, and that's probably why pitcher Mark Langston of Seattle said, "With all the home runs so far this year, I expected a slugfest."

But there was another factor that could easily affect the game in the early going. That was the starting time. Once again it was the television rights that dictated the action. So for a prime time 8:40 start on the East Coast, the game had to start at 5:40 in Oakland. And that wasn't nearly the best time of the day for baseball.

Reggie Jackson, who had played in Oakland at the

One of the hottest home-run hitters of 1987—Mark McGwire.

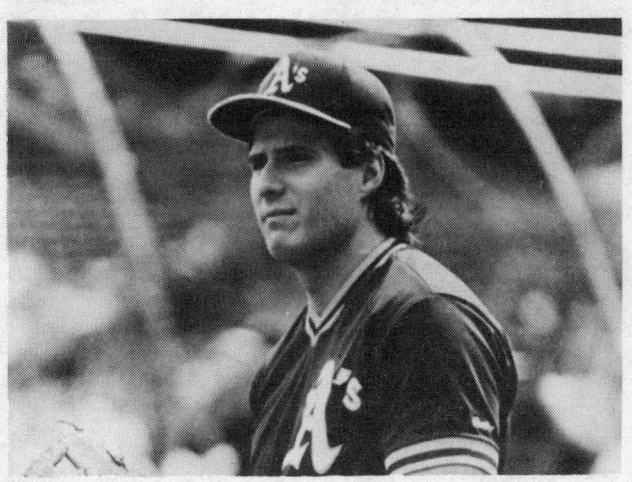

McGwire's equally hot teammate—Jose Canseco.

beginning of his career, felt that all the hitting in the world wouldn't really matter.

"Nobody's gonna get a run for a few innings because the hitters can't see the ball at that time of day," Jackson said, flat out.

Maybe the starting pitchers would be the lucky ones, pitching with the late-afternoon sun and the shadows. Mike Scott of Houston and Bred Saberhagen of Kansas City were the two hurlers with the chance to put Jackson's theory into action. Sure enough, Scott in two innings and Saberhagen in three gave up only a single hit each. And some of the hitters would confirm that they were operating at a handicap in those early innings.

"I just couldn't follow the ball at all," said Darryl Strawberry of the Mets. "It kind of snuck up on you. In fact, it was almost impossible to see."

"Without making alibis, it was awfully hard seeing the ball," confirmed veteran Mike Schmidt. "You couldn't pick up the spin or rotation. It's not the best time in the world to start a game."

Actually, the Americans had made some noise in the second. Dave Winfield doubled and Cal Ripken hit a shot that seemed ticketed for the right field line until first baseman Jack Clark of St. Louis made a leaping grab and fired to shortstop Ozzie Smith to double up Winfield. It was a big play.

Rick Sutcliff of the Cubs followed Scott to the mound and also worked two innings of one-hit ball, while Detroit's Jack Morris did the same when he replaced Saberhagen in the fourth. The Dodgers' Orel Hershiser became the third National League pitcher to work two innings and give up one hit. Mark Langston came in for the American League in the sixth and quickly retired the Nationals. At this point, neither team could use the time of day as an excuse any longer. Six innings had passed and nary a run had crossed home plate. In fact,

Darryl Strawberry.

Orel Hershiser.

there had been just five hits in the ballgame, three of them by the Nationals.

    The parade of goose eggs continued. By the time eight innings had been completed, there was still no score. In fact, it was already the longest scoreless game in All-Star history.

Six more outs and the teams would go to extra innings. And whenever a midsummer classic went to extra innings, everyone on the American League side of the ledger got a little nervous. And rightly so. The Americans had never won one that didn't end in regulation.

Dave Righetti of the Yankees was on the mound for the Americans in the top of the ninth. With one out, Montreal's Tim Raines singled. Raines, one of baseball's premier base stealers wasted no time. He broke for second, but Righetti whirled and threw to first, in effect picking Raines off. McGwire pivoted and pegged the ball toward second. Only the ball went into left field and the speedy Raines sprinted around to third.

Manager McNamara waited until the count went to 1-2 on the Phillies' Juan Samuel, a right-handed hitter, and then he brought in Toronto righty Tom Henke. The managerial wheels, as they say, were turning. But Samuel managed to lift a fly to right, where Boston's Dwight Evans settled under it. Everyone expected a play at the plate, but Raines didn't move off third.

"I knew Dwight had a good arm," Raines said. "I thought about challenging him, but there was only one out and I didn't want to take the chance."

Good thing. Evans had thrown a strike to home plate. Then, when the Giants' Jeffrey Leonard fouled to Tiger catcher Matt Nokes, the inning was over.

Now it was the Americans' turn. With Steve Bedrosian of the Phillies pitching, Dave Winfield started things off with a walk. Tony Fernandez of Toronto sacrificed him to second. Then Bedrosian walked Dwight Evans, and Seattle's Harold Reynolds came up.

Reynolds slapped a Bedrosian pitch wide of first. The

Mets' Keith Hernandez, playing off the bag, scooped the ball up and threw to second, forcing Evans. The return throw to first was wide and Bedrosian, covering the bag, was forced to make a diving catch. Seeing Bedrosian go down for the throw, Winfield rounded third, hesitated a split second, then headed for home with what would be the winning run.

Bedrosian leaped to his feet and fired the ball to catcher Ozzie Virgil. In a play reminiscent of Pete Rose crashing into Ray Fosse seventeen years earlier, Winfield slammed into Virgil. But the Atlanta catcher held on to the ball and Winfield was called out! The game would go to extra innings, still a scoreless tie.

"He ran into me hard," Virgil said of the collision.

Mets' first baseman Keith Hernandez played off the bag.

"There was a lot of beef hitting me, but I had to stay and take the hit."

Winfield looked at it this way. "I hesitated at third," the big guy said. "But when I saw him dive, I went. I would do the same thing again, except I wouldn't hesitate."

Bedrosian, the third man involved, looked at it this way. "When I saw it in the dirt I thought, 'This is it. You've got to bounce right back up and look for him.' And sure enough, he was going."

It was a big game-saving play. But now the two teams were in overtime and in the year of the home run, none of the big sluggers had yet delivered. The two clubs battled through the tenth, eleventh, and twelfth innings. Still, there was no score. For the Nationals, big Lee Smith of the Cubs had gone three impressive innings, while Henke and Jay Howell of Oakland shut down the National League hitters.

Then in the thirteenth, Ozzie Virgil opened up against Howell with a single to center. Smith, batting for himself, fanned while trying to sacrifice Virgil to second. But then Hubie Brooks slammed a single and the Cards' Willie McGee flied out. Now there were runners on first and second, two out, and Tim Raines up once more. Howell threw and Raines slammed a long drive to deep left center. It went between the outfielders and rolled to the wall. Virgil and Brooks scored, while Raines pulled up at third with a triple. The Nationals led, 2-0, at long last.

In the bottom of the inning, New York Mets left-hander Sid Fernandez entered the game and closed it out with a solid inning of relief, keeping the National Leaguers perfect in extra-inning All-Star Games. It had taken them nearly four hours and thirteen innings to win it, but they had.

And an ecstatic Tim Raines was only too happy to be the hero and the game's Most Valuable Player.

"This one ranks right up there," he said, afterward. "This is my seventh game and I hadn't gotten a hit until tonight. I told my wife coming to the game that I'd get one for her and I got three."

So the game that was supposed to resemble a home run hitting contest wound up a pitcher's battle. The unexpected can happen so often. Although the Dodgers' Orel Hershiser felt he knew the answer. "You ask why not many runs," Hershiser said. "To me it was a combination of three things. The hitters really don't know the pitchers that well, the twilight, and just plain old quality pitching."

Evidently, even in the year of the home run, the age-old baseball axiom still applied. Good pitching will always stop good hitting.

An ecstatic Tim Raines was only too happy to be the hero and the game's Most Valuable Player.

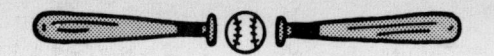

In 1950, the American League had a 12-4 advantage over the Nationals in All-Star play. By 1987, the Nationals had climbed to a 37-20-1 advantage. It had been an amazing turnaround, an overall domination so great that it is still difficult to believe. During this period, the Nationals seemed to have almost mystical powers when it came to winning All-Star Games. They won the easy ones and they won the tough ones. They came from behind numerous times, and never lost when the game went into extra innings.

Perhaps the senior circuit did have more overall superstars during this period. But that still doesn't explain the nearly total domination. The nineteen National League victories in twenty games, for instance, totally defied the law of averages. Some felt, however, that the balance of power was beginning to change in the late 1980s, the pendulum swinging back toward the American League. And about time.

Whether it swings all the way back remains to be seen. But the record will always show that the period from 1950 into the mid-1980s was a strange and unusual one in many ways. There were some great games, and very great individual efforts in an era when the All-Star Game became a nationwide, prime-time attraction. But the total domination of one league over the other is probably something that will never happen again.

Then again, never is a dangerous word, especially when you're talking about baseball, where the best advice is to stay tuned. Or as they used to say in Brooklyn a long time ago...
Wait till next year!